Using just six spices—cayenne, coriander, turmeric, mustard seed, and asafetida—ch Kahate presents 60 delicious recipes that a to prepare but deliver rich, complex flavor of these recipes use just one spice, while others layer four, five, or all six together, offering a mind-boggling, taste bud–tingling range of flavors that will instantly elevate your weeknight repertoire.

These dishes—including tons of nourishing veggies, raitas, grains, and dals—are fresh, healthy, and versatile enough to mix and match with your everyday cooking. And they feature Instant Pot variations for maximum ease. Serve up a quick lunch of Mustard Shrimp alongside a cool lettuce and citrus salad. Short on time after a busy day? Instant Pot your supper with a comforting Coconut Beef Stew. Prep a double batch of Parsi-Style Rajma on Sunday and enjoy it throughout the week—the flavors only get better over time!

With stories from Ruta's culinary life on two continents, plus vibrant, colorful photography that reflects the lively recipes within, *6 Spices, 60 Dishes* is a must-have for anyone who wants super-tasty, healthy meals that come together in a flash.

6 SPICES 60 DISHES

6 spic

Indian Recipes That Are Simple, Fresh, and Big on Taste

CHRONICLE BOOKS
SAN FRANCISCO

60 dishes

Ruta Kahate

photographs by Ghazalle Badiozamani

Library of Congress Cataloging-in-Publication Data available.

ISBN 978-1-7972-1620-1

Manufactured in China.

Design by Vanessa Dina.
Food styling by Jesse Szewczyk.
Typesetting by Frank Brayton. Typeset in Avenir.

Amazon is a registered trademark of Amazon Technologies, Inc.; Diamond Crystal Salt Co. is a registered trademark of Cargill, Incorporated; Instant Pot is a registered trademark of Instant Brands Inc.; Paul John is a registered trademark of M/s. John Distilleries Private Ltd.

10 9 8 7 6 5 4 3 2 1

Chronicle books and gifts are available at special quantity discounts to corporations, professional associations, literacy programs, and other organizations. For details and discount information, please contact our premiums department at corporatesales@chroniclebooks.com or at 1-800-759-0190.

Chronicle Books LLC
680 Second Street
San Francisco, California 94107
www.chroniclebooks.com

This book is for my intrepid little family:
my husband, Neville, and my daughters,
Mira and Lola, three amazing individuals
in their own right, yet who are always on board
for every crazy adventure I dream up.

My Crazy Culinary Journey

My father was the head of the India Government Mint, overseeing the country's vast supply of coins. Every few years, he'd be transferred to a different branch of the mint: Delhi in the north, Hyderabad in the south, Calcutta in the east, and Bombay in the west. Growing up in the four corners of India made a deep impression on me, especially since our family always dove headlong into the local cuisine.

We weren't a typical Indian family; everyone cooked at home, my father included. And my iconoclastic mother would happily break every rule of traditional Indian cooking and achieve amazing results. Many of her techniques, such as minimal intervention, flash-cooking leafy greens, and a lighter touch with spices, sauces, and oils, still inform my cooking today.

Like my brother, I learned to cook early on, but what I really wanted to do was fly. Dreaming of becoming India's first female aviator, I moved to the San Francisco Bay Area to attend a flying school. I got my pilot's license but ended up navigating the incredible food scene instead. I worked at French and Italian restaurants, ran my own Indian cooking school, led culinary tours to India, and wrote my first cookbook, *5 Spices, 50 Dishes*.

When my two little girls, Mira and Lola, were born, we decided to go on an adventure before school calendars could take over our lives. We sold our house in Oakland and moved to Goa, a tiny tropical paradise on India's west coast. There's no better place to slow down than this ex-Portuguese colony, where everything closes for the afternoon siesta. But the problem is, I don't slow down. So I started and ran six cafés of all shapes and sizes: from a one-hundred-seater casual eatery to a tapas bar shack on a stunning white-sand beach. It wasn't easy getting all the produce I needed, so I grew my own, up on a hill in my mother-in-law's village. I planted tropical things such as bananas, squash, and amaranth, but also the things I missed, such as arugula and butternut squash. Anything the pigs, peacocks, and porcupines didn't gobble up went straight to my cafés.

We ended up staying ten years in Goa, learning the local cuisine: not quite Indian, not quite Portuguese, but amazing just the same. During that time, I saw how India and its food were rapidly evolving around me. A thriving food blogger community emerged, focused on regional Indian cooking, which hadn't seen the light of day before social media. People were abandoning the big cities in droves, seeking Goa's clean air and a simple, creative lifestyle. Our neighbors included yoga teachers and cheese makers, musicians and sausage makers, writers and chocolatiers. The local fish thali lunch places and "multi-cuisine" joints were joined by vegan cafés, regional Indian eateries, and fine dining restaurants run by food professionals, both Indian and foreign. The boring liquor scene was transformed by microbreweries, small-batch gin makers, and world-class single malt whiskys like Paul John.

It was a wild ride, interrupted once again by my perpetual wanderlust. And now I'm in Milwaukee, Wisconsin, on the shores of Lake Michigan, where I run a lively little eatery called Ruta's. We serve Indian-inspired café fare to a bunch of truly amazing, appreciative customers. And as always, I'm learning. While I'm delving deeper into regional Indian food, I'm also investigating Midwestern farming communities and local produce to find that meeting point where culinary magic happens.

And, of course, I wrote this book, building on all my experiences but staying true to my tried and tested recipe: extracting great Indian flavors with minimal effort.

How lucky I am to be able to keep discovering, learning, and creating within this amazing genre!

One New Spice; a Whole New Book

In my first cookbook, *5 Spices, 50 Dishes*, I challenged the popular belief that Indian food is difficult to make. And I demonstrated how to create complex-tasting dishes using a few commonly available spices and quick-cooking techniques. *Deep flavors with minimal fuss.* This simple-yet-not-simplistic approach apparently struck a chord, judging by the response my little book received.

In the years since *5 Spices* was written, the world has gotten even smaller. Turmeric is now a household word, even being blended into smoothies. Grains common to rural India like sorghum and amaranth, coconut and sesame oils, mango and jackfruit, all kinds of beans and pulses—these are no longer exotic. Your supermarket probably stocks multiple brands of ghee, and your kitchen most likely has an Instant Pot (what my mother calls a "modern pressure cooker").

For this cookbook, I wanted to highlight a sixth spice in addition to the original five. There were so many amazing contenders, but in the end I went with asafetida because of its legendary ability to transform dishes. And also because it's now widely available in the Western world.

The mainstreaming of Indian ingredients provides a great opportunity to open things up and give you more variety in the recipes. But I also used a few non-Indian things like kale and parsnips, faves in my own home kitchen. Purists may huff, but these nutrient-dense leafy greens and roots remind me of similar vegetables in India. They respond to my techniques in the same manner as the more traditional fare—and end up tasting every bit as Indian.

Which brings me to a question I'm often asked by Westerners: Are these "authentic" Indian recipes? My answer is that every Indian home cook has their own version of any particular dish, learned from ancestors, neighbors, and even the internet. Whose version is authentic? Blood feuds have been fought over this question, because each cook is firmly convinced that their version is better and more authentic than anyone else's! To keep the peace, this cookbook includes some recipes that are traditional, and some that are updated or with a contemporary twist. Rest assured, they are all "Indian."

All in all, this new cookbook builds on the fundamentals laid down in *5 Spices, 50 Dishes* yet embraces the many changes that have occurred in India and in the West since its publication. The basic premise still holds true, because one thing didn't change and probably never will: People are still as busy as ever, juggling work and home—and *there is an enduring need for a simple, quick way to create healthy, complex-tasting meals.* This cookbook delivers on that need.

Versatility Is My Secret Sauce

While the recipes in this cookbook are unmistakably Indian, the flavors are light and fresh enough that they will seamlessly fit into your existing repertoire. That's exactly what I had in mind while writing this cookbook: to make it so accessible that people would reach for it any time, not just for special occasions.

That's kind of how I approach Indian cooking in my own home kitchen. Sure, there are days when I'll pull out all the stops and make a complex, full-on Indian spread. But most weekdays, I'll just mix and match. I might start with an Indian main—a curry, perhaps—and build a Western-style meal around it, with a green salad, broccoli, and a crusty baguette. Or I might approach it from the opposite direction: start with a pot roast and serve a raita alongside, maybe poured over steamed veggies. The possibilities are endless, and it works like a charm, adding variety (and spice) to everyday meals.

You'll get so much more out of this book if you do the same. For example, you could try the Green Bean Peanut Salad (page 44) alongside a simple roast chicken. Serve the Curry Leaf Halibut (page 140) with roasted potatoes and carrots. Or the Cauliflower Raita (page 56) as part of a chip and dip platter. You see where I'm going with this? I've sprinkled serving tips throughout to help spark some ideas. So don't overthink it; go forth and have fun, and the results will be delicious!

6 Spices, 3 Vessels

Indians adore bold flavors. Pardon me for generalizing, but I have yet to experience bland food in an Indian home, and the recipes in this cookbook follow that spirit. Although we're going to keep things quick and simple, we'll constantly aim for deep flavors—and we'll do it with 6 spices or fewer. As a mom and businesswoman, I do that every day, using a few fave spices and a couple of well-worn pans. That's not to say I don't also deploy elaborate multi-ingredient masalas; I just save those for special occasions. Using combinations of the six spices below, you can make everything in this book: dozens of balanced, complex Indian dishes.

My 6 Flavor Friends

ASAFETIDA is a dried resin extracted from the taproot of the ferrula herb. In its raw form, it has a funky and sulfurous odor, hence the nickname *devil's dung*. So why is it on our list? Because when you add asafetida to hot oil, it acquires culinary superpowers: It turns bland veggies aromatic, creates rich onion-garlic flavor without onions or garlic, and even makes beans less gassy. Asafetida is so important to cooks in India that the country imports $9 billion worth of it every year from Central Asia. In our recipes, we'll start a dish with a pinch of powdered asafetida in sizzling oil to boost umami,

complexity, and depth. Or we'll add a little to a pot of beans to make them easy to digest.

CAYENNE is what you add to make your Indian dish leap off the table, and not just in terms of heat. You get that wonderful crimson color, a smoky aroma, plus a nice endorphin rush. The granddaddy of cayenne peppers was cultivated by the Aztecs, thousands of miles away from India. Portuguese sailors brought those chile peppers to India from South America in the 1500s, and the rest, as they say, is history. Today, India is the world's largest exporter of cayenne, and most people can't imagine Indian food without it. Fun fact: For those on a diet, the heat from cayenne will make you feel full faster, so you'll eat less!

CORIANDER SEEDS are technically the fruit of the cilantro herb, but with a completely different flavor profile: nutty, lemony, and earthy. Like cumin, coriander has been around for a very long time; archeologists have found traces of it in Tutankhamun's tomb. Its flavor is most potent when the dried seeds are freshly ground, which is why I avoid store-bought ground coriander. The *type* of grind also matters; in this cookbook we'll grind our coriander seeds coarsely—that way they won't impart an undesirable brown color to the final dish. In India, coriander

seeds are commonly used in combination with cumin in garam masalas or spice mixes.

CUMIN SEEDS are probably the most widely used spice in India, thanks to their aromatic, peppery flavor. But centuries before India discovered cumin, it was already popular in ancient Greece, Rome, and Egypt—where it was also used to embalm mummies. Thankfully, we won't be doing anything that exotic here! We'll add cumin seeds to hot oil to flavor our dishes, and we'll also grind the seeds for some recipes. By the way, cumin has great digestive properties; you can brew the spice into a tea for quick gastric relief, or just chew the seeds after meals. One thing to watch out for: Cumin and caraway seeds look similar but taste *very* different.

MUSTARD SEEDS are tiny; the smallest unit of weight in ancient India was, you guessed it, one mustard seed. But they punch way above their weight in terms of their pungent, slightly bitter flavor. In our recipes, we'll toss whole mustard seeds into sizzling oil until they audibly pop (be sure to cover your pan!). That magical reaction releases and transfers the pungent flavor to the oil, and from there to the dish being cooked. As an interesting variation, we'll also grind the seeds to make an aromatic sauce. I prefer black mustard seeds, which are available on Amazon or in Indian grocery stores, but you can also substitute the commonly available yellow ones.

TURMERIC is unique; there is simply nothing else like this oddball member of the ginger family with its neon yellow hue and musky aroma that makes so many Indian dishes look and taste "Indian." Traditional cooks still use the whole root, but many Indians find the ground version convenient. In our recipes, we'll add the spice to hot oil; this cuts its astringent edge and releases its flavor and medicinal qualities. Turmeric's active ingredient, curcumin, has anti-inflammatory and antioxidant properties, which explains that *superfood* label. Scientists are now investigating the connection between India's high turmeric consumption and the country's low rate of Alzheimer's.

My 3 Trusted Kitchen Partners

I'm afflicted with wanderlust. Every few years, my family and I have made a drastic move: from Mumbai to Hong Kong to San Francisco to Oakland to Goa to our latest stop, Milwaukee. Each time we moved, I had to get a new kitchen up and running fast. And I found that I could do most of my cooking with just three vessels:

CAST-IRON SKILLET: Cooking with one of these will boost your nutritional iron. A sturdy cast-iron skillet will also sear your meat perfectly, and you can use a metal spatula to scrape up all those wonderful browned bits without worrying about ingesting toxins. That and the fact that you can transfer it to a blazing oven to finish your dish makes this workhorse a must-have.

WOK: It's not just for Asian food; Indians use a version called a kadai. A good wok is the one thing I can't live without; I can use it to make pretty much everything. From flash-cooking greens to stewing meat to even steaming rice in a pinch, this wonderful vessel is your best friend. Get a nonstick one with a large lid that does double duty on top of your cast-iron skillet.

INSTANT POT: In the "olden days," I used a stove-top pressure cooker to make short work of my curries, cook rice, and stew beans; it was a quick way to get that slow-cooked flavor. Shortening cooking time *and* preserving nutrients? My hero! And now, to have a pressure cooker that you don't have to watch is like having my knight in shining armor propose to me. The Instant Pot–friendly recipes are called out in this cookbook. Of course, you don't really need an Instant Pot for any of the recipes in this book, but if you already own one, you know how handy it is!

A Few More Ingredients and Tools

Ingredients

BROWN SUGAR: Indian cuisine uses jaggery—a type of solid molasses—to round off flavors in certain savory dishes and to sweeten some desserts. This unrefined sugar is made either from sugarcane juice or the sap of sugar and date palms. Brown sugar is a good substitute for jaggery.

CHICKPEA FLOUR OR CHANA BESAN: Chickpea flour is made from garbanzo beans, while chana besan or chana flour is made by grinding the smaller Indian black chickpea. You can use either flour in these recipes.

COOKING MEDIUMS: Indians use two basic types of cooking fats. The first is virgin, unrefined vegetable oils obtained by cold-pressing local oil-seeds: peanuts and sesame in Central India, coconut in South and West India, and mustard in North and East India. Usually a kacchi ghani or bullock-driven press extracts the oil by crushing the seeds. These flavorful oils influenced the dishes of the region, and local cuisine developed around them. In the 1980s, sunflower and other highly refined oils became popular as "heart-healthy" cooking mediums. My mother scorned these colorless oils; they didn't add any nutrition, and worse, they added no flavor. Thankfully, the trend is moving back toward using regional, cold-pressed oils, and you can find quite a few of them in your local super-market. If not, don't worry, you can always substitute canola oil in any of the recipes here.

The second cooking medium, a favorite of Indian cooking, is ghee—clarified butter made from dairy milk. Buy ghee from your supermarket or make your own using good-quality European-style unsalted butter. Melt the butter over low heat until it clarifies; the moisture will evaporate and the milk solids will settle to the bottom. Watch closely; your ghee is ready when the solids brown a bit, lending a lovely golden hue to the clear liquid. Remove from the heat and slowly pour through a fine-mesh strainer, discarding the solid bits. Stored in a covered container, ghee can be kept at room temperature for a week. Ghee has one of the most amazing flavors in the world, instantly uplifting any dish. But, by all means, replace it with canola oil in any of these recipes.

CURRY LEAVES: Fresh curry leaves have a unique flavor and no substitute, but fortunately they're readily available now. You can find them on Amazon, but you'll get a much better deal by picking up a large bag at your local Indian or Asian grocery store. Remove them from the plastic bag, spread out on paper towels, roll them up, reinsert in the bag, and refrigerate. They'll stay fresh for at least 3 weeks. Don't freeze curry leaves; they just turn black.

23

GREEN CHILES: While my recipes call for fresh chile peppers, I haven't specified the exact variety. That's because everyone's heat tolerance is different, and I don't know which ones you'll find locally. You can use jalapeño, serrano, or chile de arbol (in order of ascending heat). Other varieties may alter the flavor of the recipes. Of course, you could skip the chiles altogether, but I'd encourage you not to do that; the results won't be as good, and besides, chile peppers are simply loaded with vitamin C.

SALT: We use two kinds in this book. While Diamond Crystal kosher salt is the standard salt in my home and café kitchens, I also like to use Himalayan pink salt. This rock salt, mined in the Himalayas, is recommended by Ayurveda as one of the purest forms of salt, containing minerals and other ingredients with medicinal properties.

Tools

BLENDER: We'll use a strong blender to purée soup, crush beans, and make curry pastes. The trick to making a smooth paste in a blender is to gradually add the water or liquid called for. If you dump a whole cup of water in at once, the mixture will never blend finely; whatever you're trying to grind will just happily whip around in the jar without further breaking down.

SPICE GRINDER: I use an electric coffee grinder. It's best to reserve a grinder exclusively for spices, or your coffee will end up tasting very Indian. In a pinch, you can grind some raw rice in between coffee and spices to clean out the odors. It's best to grind your spices to order; once ground, spices quickly lose their potency and nutrients. Unless, of course, you plan on cooking a lot from this book, which I highly recommend! In that case, grinding ½ cup each of cumin [60 g] and coriander seeds [35 g] will last you a week.

PS: This helpful key highlights vegan and gluten-free recipes throughout the book and lets you know when a particular recipe can be made in the Instant Pot.

VE: Vegan

GF: Gluten-free

IP: Instant Pot–friendly

CHAPTER

1

Health-Giving Soups

Every army that invaded India brought their own soup, finding none locally. The Mughals created rich meat broths called shorba; the Portuguese made do with potato-based caldo verde; the British transmogrified a South Indian black pepper decoction into mulligatawny. Sounds desperate, but people love soup—and a separate soup course was never a part of traditional Indian cuisine. There were other things more appropriate for the hot weather: a cooling ginger lassi during the summer months, or a fiery thimbleful of rasam served with your meal to aid digestion.

But times change and cuisines evolve. Today, there are very few restaurant menus in India that don't include soups—some vaguely colonial, some vaguely Chinese, and some from the new generation of Indian chefs who are making soup a very Indian affair. Here are some of my own; enjoy them along with your meal, or as a separate course.

Curry Leaf Chicken Broth (GF/IP)

1½ lb [680 g] bony chicken parts

One 32 oz [945 ml] carton high-quality chicken broth

4 cups [945 ml] water

1 tsp minced garlic

¼ tsp ground turmeric

1 cup [140 g] chopped carrots (¼ in [6 mm] dice)

½ cup [100 g] finely chopped tomato

½ cup [100 g] red lentils, rinsed

1 tsp ground coriander

½ tsp ground cumin

1½ Tbsp sesame oil

¼ cup [35 g] finely chopped yellow onion

20 curry leaves

1½ tsp kosher salt, or more as needed

BK (before kids), I made my own chicken stock from scratch. I'd stroll down to College Avenue in Oakland to pick up ingredients. The street was lined with my favorite vendors: the butcher, the baker, and the chocolate maker; the produce market, the fishmonger, and the cheese vendor; the pasta shop and the florist. I'd get a whole organic chicken, celery and carrots, and a bottle of wine to open while the broth simmered. AK (after kids), I barely had time to breathe. So, I devised a shortcut to ensure nutrition and ease of preparation: Enhance good-quality store-bought chicken broth with actual chicken. When we moved to Goa, I discovered that my butcher sold "curry pieces" in addition to the regular cuts. These bony pieces of chicken were perfect to add body to a quick soup. Now, back in the United States, I can get chicken backs at the meat counter. They work so well to add wonderful depth to boxed broth. If you can't find chicken backs, go ahead and use drumsticks.

SERVES 4

In a medium saucepan over medium heat, combine the chicken with the broth, water, garlic, and turmeric and bring to a boil, then immediately turn the heat down and simmer for 15 minutes. Using tongs, remove the chicken, pick off any meat, and reserve it in a bowl. Discard the bones.

Return the now-enriched broth to high heat, add the carrots, tomato, lentils, coriander, and cumin, and bring to a boil. Lower the heat to a simmer, cover, and cook until the lentils are cooked and disintegrating into the soup, about 10 minutes.

While the lentils are cooking, heat the oil in a small skillet. Throw in the onion and curry leaves. Sauté over high heat until the onion turns a dark brown, 2 to 3 minutes. Add to the simmering broth, mix in the salt, add the reserved shredded chicken, and serve hot!

INSTANT POT: Add the chicken, broth, only 2 cups [475 ml] of water, garlic, and turmeric to the Instant Pot. Cook on the Soup setting for 10 minutes. Quick-release the pressure and remove the chicken using kitchen tongs. Add the carrots, tomato, lentils, coriander, and cumin. At this point you could close the lid and Pressure Cook on High for 5 minutes, or use the Sauté function to simmer the soup until the lentils are cooked and disintegrating. Proceed with the rest of the recipe, frying the curry leaves and onion in a separate skillet, and mixing everything together.

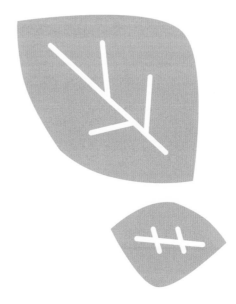

Yogurt Soup with Dill (GF)

4 cups [945 ml] water

1 Tbsp plus 1 tsp fresh lemon juice

1 cup [240 g] plain whole-milk or low-fat yogurt

3 Tbsp chana besan or chickpea flour

2 tsp kosher salt

½ tsp sugar

¼ tsp ground turmeric

¼ tsp cayenne

1 Tbsp ghee or canola oil

¼ tsp mustard seeds

¼ tsp cumin seeds

½ cup [70 g] finely chopped yellow onion

1 green chile, quartered lengthwise (optional)

¼ cup [10 g] finely chopped dill (optional, see Tip)

A warm yogurt-based brew is known as a kadhi, and there are several regional variations across India. Most are made by whisking sour yogurt and water with chana besan (see page 23), which helps emulsify the kadhi and prevents it from breaking up when heated. I add lemon juice to lend some tartness to supermarket yogurt and finish it off with a little bit of dill.

SERVES 4

In a stockpot or a wok, use a wire whisk to beat together the water, lemon juice, yogurt, chana besan, salt, sugar, turmeric, and cayenne until emulsified. Place over medium heat and just before the soup comes to a boil, turn the heat down to low and simmer for 2 minutes.

Meanwhile, in a small skillet over high heat, heat the ghee. When it is smoking, add the mustard and cumin seeds and wait for them to finish popping, just a few seconds. Add the onion and sauté until softened, 3 to 4 minutes, then add the chile and dill, if using, and cook until the leaves are softened, 2 to 3 minutes.

Slowly whisk the onion-dill mixture into the simmering soup, heat through for another minute, and serve piping-hot. Remove the chile pieces before serving, if you like.

TIP: If you're not a fan of dill, simply omit it from the recipe; you'll still get delicious results.

SERVING TIP: I like to serve this as a soup course, but you could also serve it over rice, as they do in India.

Quick and Spicy Shorba with Meatballs

(GF)

3 Tbsp ghee or canola oil

½ cup [70 g] finely chopped yellow onion

1 Tbsp grated ginger

1 Tbsp grated garlic

1 Tbsp minced green chile

½ tsp ground turmeric

1 tsp ground coriander

1 tsp ground cumin

1½ cups [300 g] finely chopped tomatoes

One 32 oz [945 ml] carton high-quality chicken broth

1 tsp kosher salt

MEATBALLS
8 oz [230 g] ground turkey or lamb

3 Tbsp minced mint

2 Tbsp minced yellow onion

1 Tbsp minced ginger

½ tsp ground cumin

½ tsp kosher salt

2 Tbsp fresh lemon juice

2 Tbsp cilantro leaves

Traditionally speaking, a shorba is a rich broth made by simmering goat or chicken bones for hours with lots of warming spices. It's delicious, and I make it once a year. But I make this updated version with store-bought chicken broth and three spices a lot more often. Quick to put together, it's light enough for summer but also has enough body to warm you up in winter. Another trick to make it work with the seasons: I use ground turkey in summer and fattier lamb during the winter.

SERVES 4

Heat the ghee in a large stockpot over medium heat and fry the onion until dark brown, 4 to 5 minutes. Add the ginger, garlic, chile, and turmeric and sauté for 1 minute, stirring constantly. Add the coriander and cumin and stir for a few seconds more. Add the tomatoes and stir, scraping up the lovely browned bits. Cover and cook over low heat until the tomatoes have all broken down and are saucy, about 5 minutes.

Transfer to a blender jar and add 1 cup [240 ml] of the chicken broth. Purée well and strain through a fine-mesh sieve back into the stockpot, pressing on the solids to extract the most out of the flavorful sauce. Add the rest of the broth and the salt to the stockpot and bring to a boil.

Meanwhile, to make the meatballs: In a large bowl, mix together the turkey, mint, onion, ginger, cumin, and salt. Roll into 16 Tbsp-size balls.

When the soup comes back to a boil, lower the heat to a simmer and slip the meatballs into the soup. Simmer the soup for 4 to 5 minutes to cook the meatballs, add the lemon juice and cilantro, and serve hot.

Haaq Soup with Brown Rice and a Boiled Egg

(GF/IP)

1 bunch (7 oz [200 g]) collard greens

½ cup [100 g] brown rice, rinsed

½ tsp asafetida

½ tsp kosher salt, or more as needed

One 32 oz [945 ml] carton high-quality chicken broth

2 cups [475 ml] water

2 Tbsp mustard oil

1 Tbsp minced green chile

6 hard-boiled eggs, each cut into 4 crosswise slices

Chile oil (recipe follows; optional)

Haaq is the Kashmiri word for greens cooked with asafetida and chiles and served over a heaping bowl of rice with yogurt on the side. In my version, I've made it more about the greens, incorporating a little bit of rice and flavoring it with all-important mustard oil. Cooked collard greens aren't the most vibrant looking, but once you've garnished it with an egg and drizzled the chile oil over, your bowl of health will look perfectly delightful.

SERVES 6

Rinse the collard greens and discard any tough stems. Tear off the leaves and stack them together. Using the point of your knife, slice the leaves vertically into four long strips. Now arrange the leaves and tender stems horizontally on your board and slice them crosswise, as thinly as you can.

Place the greens, rice, ¼ tsp of the asafetida, and the salt in a stockpot. Add the chicken broth, then pour the water into the chicken broth box and swirl it around to use up any remaining brothy goodness left in there before adding it to the stockpot. Bring to a boil, then lower the heat to a simmer, and cook, covered, until the rice is tender, about 30 minutes.

Heat the mustard oil in a small skillet until it just starts to smoke. Add the remaining ¼ tsp of asafetida and the chile and swirl the pan to toast the chile. Immediately add to the soup, using a rubber spatula to scrape up all the flavored oil, and stir.

Ladle the soup into six bowls. Fan four hard-boiled egg slices across the top of each. Drizzle with the chile oil.

continued

CHILE OIL

In a small saucepan, heat **¼ cup [60 ml] canola oil** over medium heat and swirl in **1 tsp cayenne**. Remove from the heat and let cool. You can bottle this oil and use it as a condiment to spice up other soups or even your morning eggs. This chile oil will keep at room temperature for a couple of weeks.

INSTANT POT: Rinse and prep the collard greens as instructed. Place the collard greens, rice, ¼ tsp of the asafetida, and the salt in your Instant Pot. Add the chicken broth and water and stir. Cover and set the Instant Pot to cook on the Soup setting for 20 minutes. After the pressure releases naturally, open the lid. Proceed with the rest of the recipe, frying the asafetida and chiles in a separate skillet.

CHAPTER

2

Bright Salads and Unusual Raitas

When I ran my cafés in Goa, I served salads using whatever leafy greens I could find locally. An irascible local farmer reluctantly sold me microgreens and basella. Arugula and amaranth leaves were available in the market—if you went early. Romaine and deer-tongue lettuce came from a hydroponics unit set up by an engineer recently back from the United States (thank you, Ajay!). I even grew my own, but my lovely organic greens were promptly devoured by Mr. and Mrs. Porcupine, who lived nearby (my heritage red rice met a similar fate at the beaks of the resident peacock clan). It wasn't easy, and the hot climate didn't help.

Thankfully, not all salads need greens, and all my creations were popular with my café customers. Here are some salads, with and without greens, and some raitas, which are basically salads with yogurt.

Green Bean Peanut Salad (VE/GF)

A basket of market-fresh beans (13 oz [370 g])

1 Tbsp peanut oil

½ tsp mustard seeds

¼ tsp asafetida

½ cup [70 g] roasted peanuts

3 Tbsp fresh lemon juice

1 tsp kosher salt

1 tsp sugar

I like to make this recipe with any type of fresh beans I find in the farmers' market: green beans, French beans, Chinese long beans, purple beans. Sometimes I'll even combine varieties for a vibrant mix of colors. The peanuts are there to add a nice, unexpected crunch, so grind them coarsely. I'd probably get more even results by chopping the peanuts on my cutting board, but life's too short to go chasing after peanuts that fly off the counter. So I use my spice grinder, pulsing just until I have the texture I want.

SERVES 4

String the beans if necessary. Cut the beans into 1 in [2.5 cm] diagonal slices to create diamond shapes.

Heat the oil in a large cast-iron skillet over medium heat. When it's very hot, add the mustard seeds and let them finish popping. In quick succession, add the asafetida and then the chopped beans. Toss well, cover, and steam the beans until tender but still bright green, about 4 minutes. Take off the heat, transfer to a bowl, and let cool.

Using a spice grinder, pulse the peanuts until coarsely ground. Add the lemon juice, salt, sugar, and crushed peanuts and toss well. Serve at room temperature.

> **SERVING TIP:** I like to serve this when I roast a whole chicken. I also serve it when I make Hong Kong–style stir-fried curried noodles with vegetables and pork!

Tricolor Salad (VE/GF)

1 large carrot

1 large green bell pepper

½ head green cabbage

3 Tbsp canola or sesame oil

1½ tsp mustard seeds

¼ cup [35 g] raw or toasted cashews

½ tsp ground turmeric

¼ tsp asafetida

2 Tbsp minced cilantro leaves

1 Tbsp fresh lemon juice

1 tsp sugar

1 tsp Himalayan pink salt

Here's a hearty salad that makes a great side or a perfect office lunch. A crunchy texture is desirable, so be sure to heat the vegetables just until their rawness dissipates, not until they wilt. A simple way to get good results is to shred the cabbage thinly and similarly slice the green pepper. Once they're in the wok, toss continuously, not allowing the vegetables to sweat or steam.

SERVES 4 TO 6

Peel the carrot and shred it on the large holes of a box grater—you should have about 1 cup [140 g] shredded. Julienne the green pepper thinly. Very finely slice the cabbage—you want about 3 cups [180 g] of thin ribbons. Use a mandoline if you have one.

Heat the oil in a wok over medium-high heat until smoking. Add the mustard seeds and cashews. As soon as the seeds are done popping, add the turmeric, asafetida, and green pepper and toss well. Then add the cabbage and toss for about 3 minutes. Don't let the cabbage sweat or scorch—keep tossing over high heat until it just begins to soften but is still plenty crunchy. Then add the carrot, toss, and remove from the heat.

Add the cilantro, lemon juice, sugar, and salt and mix well. Serve warm, at room temperature, or cold.

SERVING TIP: I like to keep a big batch of this in the refrigerator to pack for quick office or school lunches. I'll also often make a blender full of a protein-packed smoothie (almond butter + bananas + oat milk) to send alongside the salad.

Jicama and Mango Salad (VE/GF)

½ cup [100 g] chopped jicama
(½ in [13 mm] dice)

½ cup [70 g] chopped mango
(½ in [13 mm] dice)

½ cup [100 g] chopped tomato
(½ in [13 mm] dice)

½ cup [70 g] chopped red onion
(½ in [13 mm] dice)

½ cup [20 g] chopped
cilantro leaves

2 Tbsp fresh lemon juice

1 tsp kosher salt

1 tsp sugar

1 Tbsp canola oil

½ tsp mustard seeds

¼ tsp asafetida

¼ tsp ground turmeric

3 cups [60 g] mixed baby greens

Even though it's a root, jicama has an almost fruit-like texture. Crunchy like a crisp pear or water chestnut, it has a nutty flavor that goes superbly with the mango in this recipe. After you've dressed the salad with the hot oil dressing, allow it to cool a bit. Once cool, you can add the baby greens without fear of them wilting.

SERVES 4

In a large bowl, mix together the jicama, mango, tomato, onion, cilantro, lemon juice, salt, and sugar.

Heat the oil in a small skillet over high heat. Add the mustard seeds and, as soon as they are done popping, add the asafetida and turmeric and immediately pour it over the salad. Allow to cool before adding the mixed greens. Toss well and serve.

> **TIP:** The dressed salad can be made up to a day ahead, but add the greens just before serving.

> **SERVING TIP:** I like to serve this as a light supper alongside a charcuterie platter.

Mung Sprouts Salad (VE/GF)

3 cups [350 g] sprouted mung beans (see page 103)

½ cup [120 ml] water

½ tsp kosher salt

2 cups [40 g] baby spinach

½ cup [70 g] finely chopped red onion

½ cup [100 g] finely chopped tomato

¼ cup [5 g] cilantro leaves

1 tsp minced green chile

½ tsp Himalayan pink salt

2 Tbsp mustard oil

1 tsp mustard seeds

½ tsp asafetida

10 curry leaves

¼ cup [20 g] dried, shredded, unsweetened coconut

1 Tbsp fresh lemon juice

Sprouts are an indispensable part of my Marathi community's diet. We sprout everything—mung beans, fenugreek seeds, black-eyed peas, even peanuts. Germination breaks down some of the starch, making more nutrients available. Beans become less gassy and easier to digest. In Ayurvedic speak, sprouting releases the *life force* of the ingredient, which just makes me feel so healthy while eating my sprouts!

SERVES 4 TO 6

Place the sprouts, water, and kosher salt in a small pan. Cover and steam the sprouts lightly over medium heat, about 4 minutes. Drain any remaining water, transfer the sprouts to a medium bowl, and let cool. Add the spinach, onion, tomato, cilantro, chile, and pink salt to the sprouts and mix well.

Heat the oil in a small skillet over high heat. Add the mustard seeds, and as soon as they're done popping, add the asafetida and curry leaves. The leaves will toast almost immediately. Pour this hot oil dressing over the sprout salad in the bowl. Add the coconut and lemon juice and mix well.

Serve at room temperature or cold. It will keep, tightly covered in the refrigerator, for 2 to 3 days.

> **SERVING TIP:** I like to serve this as part of a larger vegetarian meal alongside grilled vegetable patties and a sweet and spicy chutney.

Black Grape Raita (GF)

½ cup [80 g] seedless
black grapes

¼ cup [40 g] seedless
green grapes

1½ cups [360 g] plain
whole-milk or low-fat yogurt

1 tsp Himalayan pink salt

1 tsp sugar

¼ tsp ground cumin

¼ cup [35 g] minced
red onion

1 Tbsp finely chopped mint

Fruit naturally lends itself to yogurt-based raitas. Adding slightly sulfurous Himalayan pink salt gives the raita a special Indian flavor, and crunchy grapes provide the finishing touch for a perfect summer relish.

SERVES 4

Quarter each grape. In a medium bowl, whisk the yogurt with the salt, sugar, and cumin until smooth. Add the grapes, onion, and mint to the yogurt, mix well, and refrigerate the raita until ready to serve. Serve chilled. This will keep in the refrigerator, in a covered container, for a couple of days.

SERVING TIP: I like to serve this as an accompaniment to spicy chicken skewers at a barbecue.

Avocado Raita (GF)

½ cup [120 g] plain whole-milk or low-fat yogurt

½ cup [120 ml] water

¼ cup [30 g] finely chopped shallot

2 Tbsp finely chopped cilantro leaves

1 tsp Himalayan pink salt, or more as needed

¼ tsp ground cumin

2 perfectly ripe medium avocados

1 Tbsp toasted flax seeds

Sprinkle of cayenne

Here's a light summer raita that takes literally minutes to create. Although it makes a wonderful dip, it's not an Indian guacamole—so don't mash the avocado! Instead, score the flesh into cubes and carefully scoop them out using a spoon.

SERVES 4

In a medium serving bowl, whisk the yogurt and water together until smooth. Add the shallot, cilantro, salt, and cumin and whisk again to combine well. Taste and adjust the salt as needed. Pink salt tends to be less salty than kosher salt, so you may need more.

Halve each avocado, remove the seeds, and score the flesh of each half to mark 1 in [2.5 cm] squares. Using a spoon, scoop out the pieces of avocado and transfer to the bowl of prepared yogurt. Gently stir the avocado into the yogurt, taking care not to mash it.

Just before serving, sprinkle the flax seeds and then the cayenne over the raita. Serve immediately.

TIP: Avocado discolors quickly once cut, so if possible, try to make this dish "just in time."

SERVING TIP: You could serve this raita like a salad, over a bed of lettuce, or as a dip with toasts.

Bittersweet Raita (GF)

2 medium karela or Asian bitter melons (see Tip)

2 Tbsp canola oil

1 cup [240 g] plain yogurt, preferably whole-milk

¼ tsp ground cumin

1 tsp Himalayan pink salt

2 Tbsp minced red onion

You can find karela, or bitter melons, at Indian grocery stores, their skin covered with ridges and bumps. When my daughters were little, they'd eat all kinds of vegetables, but this one was a challenge—until the day I deep-fried disks of karela into thin, crispy little chips. The bitterness gave way to a caramelized sweetness, and the girls have loved karela ever since. Here I sprinkle those chips on top of whisked yogurt for a delightful raita.

SERVES 4

Using a mandoline or a very sharp knife, slice the melon into very thin rounds.

Heat a cast-iron skillet over low to medium heat and then add the oil. Add the karela slices and sauté until each slice is crisp and brown on both sides. This will take at least 10 to 15 minutes. Be patient. Don't crank up the heat to hasten the process; you want sweetly caramelized, not bitter and burnt, karela!

In a medium serving bowl, whisk the yogurt with the cumin and salt until smooth and then mix in the onion. When you're ready to serve, top the yogurt with the crisp slices of karela, mixing them in only at the table. Serve at room temperature or cold.

> **TIP:** The smooth-skinned Asian bitter melon is more easily available; feel free to substitute for karela.

> **SERVING TIP:** I like to serve this as an unusual dip on an appetizer platter.

Cauliflower Raita (GF)

1½ heaping cups [200 g] riced cauliflower (see Tip)

½ cup [120 ml] water

½ cup [120 ml] plain whole-milk or low-fat yogurt

3 Tbsp dried, shredded, unsweetened coconut

2 Tbsp minced cilantro leaves

1 Tbsp grated green chile (see Tip)

2 tsp kosher salt

1 tsp sugar

I'm always a little underwhelmed by cauliflower, finding it lacking in flavor. But since it is a cruciferous vegetable—and I include one of those almost daily in our diet—it does its rounds in my kitchen. Here, simply steaming the cauliflower and then whisking it into spiced yogurt really elevates the vegetable.

SERVES 4

Place the cauliflower and water together in a pan over medium heat and bring to a boil. Turn the heat down to low, cover, and steam the cauliflower for 2 minutes. Remove from the heat, uncover, and let cool completely. Drain and discard any remaining water.

In a medium bowl, whisk the yogurt with the coconut, cilantro, chile, salt, and sugar. Add the cooled cauliflower to the mixture. Refrigerate to cool further, at least 10 minutes, before serving.

> **TIPS:** To rice cauliflower, simply grate the cauliflower with a box grater. Or you could throw a few large pieces of cauliflower into your food processor and pulse until it is evenly and finely chopped.
>
> Wear gloves while grating the chile.
>
> **SERVING TIP:** I like serving this with slices of cold roast beef tenderloin; add the Alluring Asparagus (page 90) for a fancy meal.

3

Vegetables: Leaf, Fruit, Flower, Root

My mother loved experimenting in the kitchen. The same old vegetables in the same old seasonal rotation simply bored her. She banned potatoes, claiming they were for lazy cooks who didn't value nutrition. Instead, she served us all manner of interesting leaves, stems, fruits, flowers, and roots. Along with spinach and lettuce, we ate amaranth, mustard greens, and bitter melon leaves. Beets were supplemented with pretty lotus root or weird-looking elephant yam. We liked vegetable "fruit" like tomatoes and eggplant, and we *loved* drumsticks—the stick-shaped fruit of the moringa tree. Actual fruit like mango, jackfruit, and pineapple went into chutneys, dals, and curries. And we ate lots of flowers: fried pumpkin flowers and dishes made from the huge purple banana blossom or the tiny white flowers of the bitter neem tree.

Without getting too exotic, this chapter features a wide range of vegetables. After all, variety makes life—and dinner—a lot more interesting!

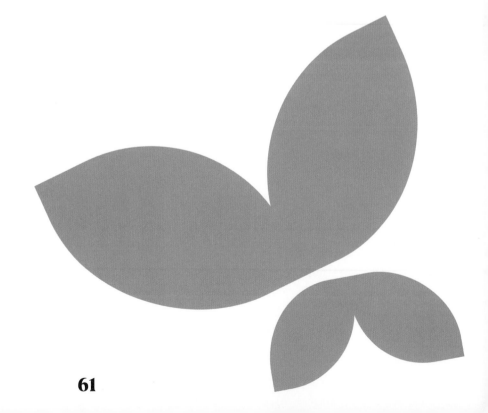

Silken Eggplant with Coconut

(VE/GF)

1 large globe eggplant (about 1 lb [455 g])

¼ cup [60 ml] canola oil, or more as needed

1 tsp ground coriander

½ tsp kosher salt

¼ tsp ground turmeric

½ cup [70 g] chopped red onion

¼ cup [10 g] chopped cilantro leaves

1 Tbsp minced green chile

¼ cup [20 g] dried, shredded, unsweetened coconut

And my baby cooks her eggplant about nineteen different ways. Sometimes I just have it raw with mayonnaise. If Michael Franks's whimsical lyrics were a recipe, you'd end up with an inedible dish! Eggplant is one of those vegetables that should *always* be well done. Otherwise it can taste nasty and, as a member of the nightshade family, even be mildly toxic. This recipe will result in a delicate, perfectly cooked eggplant dish, true to its name. A cast-iron skillet works best because it retains heat so well; the eggplant cooks all the way through while browning perfectly.

SERVES 4 TO 6

Slice the eggplant into ½ in [13 mm] thick slices. Heat a cast-iron skillet over medium-high heat and add the oil; add more oil if necessary to fully coat the pan. Fry the eggplant in batches. Spread the slices in an even layer in the pan and cook until brown on one side, about 2 minutes, then turn each slice over and cook the other side another couple of minutes, until browned all over and soft and silky.

Place the browned slices in overlapping layers in a shallow serving bowl and mash slightly, cutting gently with a fork into the eggplant, being careful not to reduce it to a pulp. Sprinkle with the coriander, salt, and turmeric, then top with the onion, cilantro, chile, and finally the coconut. Serve right away, or you could even prepare it ahead of time and refrigerate.

SERVING TIP: I like to serve this with a nice chunky soup such as minestrone.

Brussels Sprouts with Fried Red Lentils

(VE/GF)

12 oz [340 g] Brussels sprouts, halved lengthwise

1 cup [240 ml] hot water

2 Tbsp peanut oil

½ tsp cumin seeds

1 Tbsp red lentils

1 cup [140 g] sliced yellow onion (¼ in [6 mm] slices)

1 green chile, cut into thick rounds

2 tsp minced garlic

¼ tsp asafetida

1 tsp kosher salt

1 cup [40 g] chopped cilantro leaves

From the time they were toddlers, my daughters have liked their veggies, even those shunned by other tiny tots. Take Brussels sprouts; like their cousins cauliflower, cabbage, and broccoli, these crucifers have an odor problem. An open bag of Brussels sprouts is enough to put any child off; boiling them fills the entire house with sulfurous fumes. I'm careful to avoid releasing any off-putting aromas while working with these vegetables. Instead, I use the magical powers of asafetida to degas the crucifers, and sauté them in flavored oils to turn them into delicious vegetables anyone will like—even kids.

SERVES 6

Place the Brussels sprouts in a cast-iron skillet. Pour in the hot water and place over high heat. Cover and steam the sprouts until tender but not mushy, 3 to 5 minutes. Drain any remaining water and transfer the sprouts to a bowl.

Reheat the dry skillet over high heat and add the oil. When the oil is very hot, add the cumin seeds and lentils—both will toast almost immediately, so be ready to add the onion right away. Sauté the onion until softened slightly, about 1 minute. Add the chile, garlic, and asafetida, and sauté for another minute.

Add the steamed Brussels sprouts and salt and toss well. Turn the heat down to low and let the flavors meld and the sprouts brown a bit, 2 to 3 minutes. Stir in the cilantro and remove from the heat. Serve hot or at room temperature.

SERVING TIP: I like to serve this with honey-glazed pork chops.

Sweet Potato and Broccoli Curry (VE/GF)

½ small sweet potato
(about 4 oz [115 g])

½ head broccoli
(about 4 oz [115 g])

½ small zucchini
(about 4 oz [115 g])

½ cup [120 ml] water

2 tsp coriander seeds

½ cup [100 g] finely
chopped tomato

½ cup [70 g] finely
chopped yellow onion

1 Tbsp minced garlic

½ tsp ground turmeric

¼ tsp cayenne

2 Tbsp coconut oil

¼ tsp cumin seeds

¼ tsp mustard seeds

One 13½ oz [385 g] can
coconut milk, shaken well

2 green chiles,
quartered lengthwise

1 tsp brown sugar

1 tsp kosher salt

2 Tbsp finely chopped
cilantro leaves

Here's a wholesome curry full of veggie goodness that also packs a little heat to chase away winter blues. A fixture on my café menus, this dish was a hit with my customers, and not just the vegans. By first steaming the vegetables and then adding a simple spice blend, you'll have a complex-tasting curry on your table in under 20 minutes.

Don't let the longish list of ingredients furrow your brow; the dish comes together with minimal effort. For simplicity, I've separated the steps into four parts: prep the veggies, toast the spices, grind them with the tomato and garlic, and then put everything together.

SERVES 4

Cut the sweet potato, broccoli, and zucchini into large chunks, about 1½ in [4 cm] pieces. In a medium pan with a lid, bring the water to a boil. Add the sweet potato, cover, turn the heat down to medium, and steam until tender, about 3 minutes. With a slotted spoon, transfer the sweet potato to a plate and cover. Now add the broccoli and zucchini to the simmering water, cover, and steam until fork-tender, another 3 minutes. Turn off the heat, return the sweet potato to the pan, and set aside, keeping it covered, while you get the masala ready. Do not discard any water remaining in the pan.

In a dry skillet over low heat, toast the coriander seeds until lightly browned, 2 minutes. Cool slightly and finely grind in a clean spice grinder. In a blender jar, combine the tomato, onion, garlic, turmeric, cayenne, and the freshly ground coriander; blend to a smooth purée.

In the same skillet, heat the oil over medium-high heat. When the oil starts rippling, add the cumin and mustard seeds. After they're done sputtering, add the tomato-onion purée and cook, stirring occasionally, until the masala paste has thickened slightly and smells fragrant, 3 to 4 minutes.

continued

66

Turn the heat down to low, add the coconut milk and chiles, and whisk to incorporate fully. Stir in the sugar and salt and bring to a simmer. Immediately transfer this sauce to the pan with the vegetables. Do not stir, or you may end up with an unattractive mash! Instead, shake the pan gently to mix.

Simmer gently until heated through, 3 to 4 minutes. It's best not to let the curry come to a boil, as the coconut milk may curdle and there goes your beautiful dish!

Garnish with the cilantro and serve.

SERVING TIP: I like to serve this with steamed rice and cranberry chutney.

Mustard and Cilantro Greens with Burnt Onions

(VE option/GF)

2 Tbsp ghee or canola oil

1 tsp mustard seeds

8 curry leaves

¼ tsp asafetida

1 medium red onion, thinly sliced

1 Tbsp minced garlic

½ tsp ground turmeric

1½ tsp ground coriander

1 tsp ground cumin

1 bunch (10½ oz [300 g]) mustard greens, finely chopped

1 bunch (3 oz [85 g]) cilantro, finely chopped

1 green chile, quartered lengthwise

½ tsp kosher salt

I love greens and cook them every day. To keep things interesting, I rotate my greens depending on where I've last shopped. From the neighborhood supermarket: spinach, kale, mustard greens, turnip greens, beet greens. From the farmers' market: dandelion, watercress, purslane, radish greens, amaranth. From the Asian grocery store: bok choy, choi sum, gai lan, pea shoots, water spinach. With such variety readily available these days, there really is no excuse not to eat your greens. I usually flash-cook them simply with garlic and a flavorful oil like mustard. Sometimes, though, I'll go the extra mile and make something special like this recipe.

SERVES 4

Heat the ghee in a wok over medium-high heat until smoking. Add the mustard seeds, and when they're done sputtering, quickly add the curry leaves and asafetida. The curry leaves will get toasted instantly; immediately add the onion and sauté until it is very dark brown, but not burned, 2 to 3 minutes.

Add the garlic, turmeric, coriander, and cumin, and stir for 1 minute. Throw in the mustard greens, cilantro, chile, and salt and mix well. Cover, turn the heat down to medium, and cook until all the greens have cooked down, about 5 minutes. Serve warm.

> **SERVING TIP:** I like to serve this with any meal, but I love it with a pork loin roast glazed with a sweet and sour sauce.

Stuffed Anaheim Peppers

(VE/GF)

4 large Anaheim peppers

½ cup [60 g] chana besan or chickpea flour

1 tsp white or brown sesame seeds

½ tsp ground turmeric

½ tsp cumin seeds

½ tsp ground coriander

½ tsp kosher salt

½ tsp brown sugar

¼ tsp cayenne

½ cup [20 g] chopped cilantro leaves

2 Tbsp water

1 Tbsp fresh lemon juice

3 Tbsp sesame oil

Although chiles were introduced to India by the Portuguese as recently as the 1500s, you'd think they originated in India. With a cuisine so steeped in chiles, and the sheer variety grown all over the country, it's easy to be fooled. From the incendiary bhoot jhalokia of Nagaland to the fiery Guntur of Andhra Pradesh to the smoky, highly pigmented Kashmiri of its namesake Himalayan state of Kashmir, each variety has its uses and devotees. This recipe makes mild Anaheim peppers the star of the dish. You can even serve it as a main course for the vegetarians among your guests.

SERVES 2 AS A MAIN OR 4 AS A SIDE

Wash and wipe dry the peppers, keeping the stem intact if possible. Make a long vertical slit in each of the peppers and shake out any seeds.

Heat a cast-iron skillet over medium heat and add the chana besan and sesame seeds. Stir continuously with a wire whisk until the besan smells nutty and is toasted to a very light golden brown, about 2 minutes. Immediately scrape into a bowl and rinse and wipe out the skillet.

To the bowl with the chana besan, add the turmeric, cumin seeds, coriander, salt, sugar, and cayenne, and stir to combine well. Add the cilantro, water, and lemon juice and stir to make a rough paste. Stuff this paste into the prepped peppers, dividing the mixture evenly among all four peppers.

Reheat the skillet over medium heat and add the oil. When the oil is warmed up well, add the peppers, being careful to avoid any splattering oil. Cover and cook until browned on one side, 3 to 4 minutes. Uncover and use tongs to flip each pepper, cover, and continue cooking, another 3 to 4 minutes. The peppers will have browned and softened and the filling cooked through. Serve immediately or at room temperature.

> **SERVING TIP:** I like to serve this as a vegetarian main dish with a roasted beet, orange, and feta salad.

Turnips with Green Garlic

(VE/GF)

2 Tbsp mustard oil

½ tsp ground turmeric

¼ tsp asafetida

1 tsp ground cumin

1 tsp ground coriander

2 Tbsp chopped green garlic

1 Tbsp grated ginger

2 large turnips, cut into
1 in [2.5 cm] cubes

1 cup [40 g] chopped cilantro
leaves and tender stems

½ cup [60 g] freshly shelled peas

1 green chile, quartered
lengthwise

1 tsp kosher salt

¼ tsp sugar

Who knew that there are more than twenty varieties of turnip: from the white globe, to the golden ball, to the bright red radish look-alikes, some even deviating from the usual round shape and growing long like a carrot. I favor the commonly available purple-topped white ones. In the spring, you can find small, tender turnips at the farmers' market. Keep an eye out for green garlic and early sweet peas too. Add one more green—cilantro—and you'll have a fresh, bright, and happy dish that heralds summer.

SERVES 4

Heat the oil in a wok over medium heat. Add the turmeric and asafetida first, and then follow with the cumin, coriander, garlic, and ginger and stir for about 30 seconds. Add the cubed turnips, cilantro, peas, chile, salt, and sugar and toss well. Cover tightly and braise until the turnips are crisp-tender, about 3 minutes. Serve hot.

SERVING TIP: I like to serve this with simple oven-roasted chicken thighs.

Fried Plantains with Coconut (GF)

---

4 yellow plantains
(about 14 oz [400 g]; see Tip)

2 Tbsp canola oil

2 Tbsp ghee or butter

½ tsp ground turmeric

1 tsp kosher salt

1 cup [115 g] minced shallots

1 tsp finely grated garlic

1 green chile (optional)

2 Tbsp dried, shredded,
unsweetened coconut

1 Tbsp chana besan or
chickpea flour

The main difference between plantains and bananas is that the former are starchier and cooked as a vegetable; they are way too astringent to be eaten raw. You'll find green, yellow, and black plantains in the supermarket. The green ones are unripe, yellow are just ripe, and the black ones are very ripe and sweet, best used in desserts. For this recipe we want the yellow ones.

SERVES 6

Rinse and dry the plantains using a clean kitchen towel. Slice on the diagonal into ½ in [13 mm] thick slices. Heat the oil and ghee together in a cast-iron skillet over medium heat until pretty hot. Add the turmeric, give it a stir, and add the sliced plantains and salt. Toss well, cover, and cook over medium heat until the plantains are crisp-tender, about 5 minutes.

Turn the heat down to low and add the shallots, garlic, and chile (if using). Sauté, uncovered, until the shallots have softened, about 2 minutes.

In a small bowl, stir the coconut and besan together. Add to the skillet and stir continuously until the besan is toasted, about 2 minutes. Be careful, as besan tends to burn quickly.

Serve warm or at room temperature.

> **TIP:** Don't bother peeling plantains before cooking; it's easy to take the peel off the few slices on the plate. Peeling a whole unripe plantain is a struggle that requires wearing gloves or coating your hands with oil to avoid the itchiness, as the ancients did.

> **SERVING TIP:** I like to serve this with hearty dishes such as pulled pork or Parsi-Style Rajma (page 100).

Young Jackfruit Curry (GF)

One 14 oz [400 g] can organic young jackfruit, drained

1½ cups [360 ml] water

¾ tsp ground turmeric

2 Tbsp peanut oil

½ tsp cumin seeds

¼ tsp asafetida

1 Tbsp grated ginger

2 tsp ground coriander

½ tsp cayenne

½ tsp ground cumin

½ cup [100 g] chopped tomato

½ cup [120 g] plain whole-milk or low-fat yogurt, whisked

1 tsp kosher salt

¼ cup [10 g] chopped cilantro leaves

I'm a bit bemused by jackfruit's newfound fame as a vegan superfood. Wherever I've lived in India, from Calcutta in the east, to Mumbai in the west, to Goa on the coast, I've never been far from the alien-looking jackfruit tree, with its many clusters of gigantic spiky fruit growing straight out of the trunk. Indians turn the unripe fruit into curries, but they get really excited when the fruit ripens, offering an abundance of sweet yellow flesh that can feed an army. From a Western perspective, unripe jackfruit has a neutral flavor and stringy texture that makes it a great plant-based alternative to meat. This being an Indian cookbook, here's a robust curry that's perfect for vegetarians and can almost convince carnivores that they are eating the real thing.

SERVES 4

Transfer the drained jackfruit to a small saucepan and cover with the water. Add ¼ tsp of the turmeric and boil the jackfruit for 5 minutes.

Heat the oil in a wok over medium-high heat until it starts smoking, and then add the cumin seeds. As soon as the seeds are done sputtering, add the asafetida and then the ginger. Stir constantly until the ginger is browned, then add the remaining ½ tsp of turmeric, along with the coriander, cayenne, and cumin. Stir for about 30 seconds, then add the tomato and cook until saucy, about 5 minutes, stirring often. Whisk in the yogurt and salt and cook for 1 minute more.

Using a slotted spoon, pick out the jackfruit from the water and add it to the tomato-yogurt sauce. Mix well so the jackfruit is well coated in the sauce. Let cook over medium heat for 5 minutes. Stir in the cilantro.

Serve warm.

SERVING TIP: I like to serve this with Fluffy Millet with Cashews (page 123) or lemony couscous.

Zucchini with Coriander Two Ways

(VE/GF)

2 large firm zucchini

3 Tbsp sesame oil

¼ tsp ground turmeric

1 tsp kosher salt

1 tsp ground coriander

½ cup [20 g] minced cilantro (a.k.a. coriander) leaves

There are any number of thin-skinned summer squashes in India, all known as gourds. Opo squash is called bottle gourd because it resembles one. There's the undulating snake gourd, the prickly spine gourd, and several others named after their appearance, such as ash gourd, sponge gourd, and ridge gourd. All share a common quality: a high water content, or what my husband calls "translucence." For this reason you have to be careful not to overcook them and end up with unattractive mushy results. Zucchini or pattypan squash both work very well in this simple recipe. But do make sure to cook over pretty high heat so the vegetable braises rather than steams.

SERVES 4

Halve each zucchini lengthwise and then cut crosswise into ¼ in [6 mm] thick half-moons.

Heat a cast-iron skillet over medium-high heat. Add the oil and turmeric, and stir for a few seconds. Add the zucchini, toss well, and spread them out so they fry more than sweat in the skillet, flipping occasionally until the zucchini are well browned but not mushy, 5 to 7 minutes. Sprinkle with the salt and coriander, followed by the cilantro leaves. Serve immediately.

> **SERVING TIP:** I like to serve this with spicy beef stir-fried with black pepper and orange peel.

Golden Root Veggies Stir-Fry

(VE/GF)

2 or 3 sunchokes (3½ oz [100 g])

2 or 3 parsnips (3½ oz [100 g])

2 or 3 golden beets (3½ oz [100 g])

1 chunk (3½ oz [100 g]) daikon

2 Tbsp canola oil

½ tsp cumin seeds

¼ tsp mustard seeds

¼ tsp asafetida

10 curry leaves

1 green chile, quartered lengthwise

1 Tbsp minced ginger

1 tsp kosher salt

½ tsp ground turmeric

½ tsp cayenne

½ tsp brown sugar

1 Tbsp fresh lemon juice

Here's a dish that looks as good as it tastes, or is it the other way around? Sunchokes, parsnips, golden beets, and daikon—strange, knobbly looking things you'd probably walk past in the vegetable aisle—come together to make a beautiful dish. You may be aware that sunchokes and daikon have a reputation for, um, gassiness. But fear not, you have the dual digestive dynamos—asafetida and ginger—on your side.

SERVES 4

Peel the sunchokes, parsnips, beets, and daikon and cut into ½ in [13 mm] cubes. The next step will take only a few seconds, so have everything handy before you heat your wok.

Heat the oil in a wok over medium heat until smoking, slide the wok off the burner, and add the cumin and mustard seeds. When they're done sputtering, add the asafetida, curry leaves, chile, and ginger and slide the wok back onto the burner. As soon as the curry leaves are toasted, add the chopped root veggies. Toss, add the salt, turmeric, cayenne, and sugar, and toss again. Cover and cook over medium-high heat, uncovering and tossing only a couple of times, until the vegetables are browned and fork-tender, about 10 minutes total. Add the lemon juice and toss again well. Serve hot or at room temperature.

> **SERVING TIP:** I like to serve this with my Sunday pot roast (which I make in my Instant Pot!).

Farmer Baby Stir-Fry

(VE/GF)

4½ oz [130 g] baby eggplant (about 4)

4 oz [115 g] baby okra (about 1 cup)

4¼ oz [120 g] sugar snap peas (about 1 cup)

2 Tbsp sesame oil

½ tsp mustard seeds

¼ tsp cumin seeds

¼ tsp asafetida

¼ tsp ground turmeric

¼ tsp cayenne

1 tsp kosher salt

1 tsp brown sugar

I've always grown vegetables in my backyard, but during my ten years in Goa, I went all out. My "farm" was a sloping piece of land up on a hill in my mother-in-law's village. I grew all kinds of organic produce for my cafés, and bananas and red rice for my family. Opo squash climbed every red laterite stone wall it could find; running out of ways to use them, I simply sold or gave them away. Okra and eggplant were also hyper-prolific, but I learned a little trick to manage their sheer number: harvest them young! Here's a wonderful stir-fry to use up your garden bounty early, or perhaps you've just gone to the farmers' market and found a farmer like me: nipping her produce in the bud, so to speak.

SERVES 4

Cut each baby eggplant in half lengthwise. Keep the baby okra whole. You may not find any strings on the sugar snap peas if they are as tender as the rest of the veggies. Otherwise, string them.

Heat the oil in a wok over medium heat until very hot. Add the mustard and cumin seeds—they should splutter. In quick succession throw in the asafetida, turmeric, cayenne, and the vegetables. Add the salt and sugar and toss well. Cover and cook over medium-high heat, uncovering and tossing two or three times during the cooking process, until the eggplant is soft, 3 to 4 minutes. Do not overcook—tender vegetables like these don't need more than a few minutes in the wok. Also, make sure to cook them over pretty high heat, otherwise they run the risk of becoming unappetizingly mushy, instead of meltingly tender. Serve warm.

SERVING TIP: I like to serve this with grilled Italian sausage.

Tropical Winter Peas

(VE option/GF)

1 cup [120 g] fresh or frozen peas, thawed slightly if frozen

1 cup [240 ml] water

3 Tbsp ghee or canola oil

½ tsp cumin seeds

1 cup [140 g] chopped yellow onion

1 Tbsp grated ginger

1 Tbsp grated garlic

1 Tbsp minced green chile

1 tsp ground cumin

1 tsp ground coriander

½ tsp ground turmeric

½ cup [100 g] chopped tomato

1½ tsp kosher salt, or more as needed

1 Tbsp fresh lemon juice

Peas are a *winter* crop in India; summers there are much too hot and humid for these delicate legumes. The seeds are sown between September and November, depending on the region, and by December every vegetable market has mountains of plump peas in their pods. In the United States and other Western countries, peas are a summer crop, of course. But all kinds of peas, summer or winter, fresh or frozen, work well in this aromatic curry.

SERVES 4

In a blender, coarsely grind the peas with half the water and set aside.

Heat the ghee in a wok over medium heat until smoking, then add the cumin seeds. Within a few seconds the cumin will stop sputtering—add the onion and sauté until browned well, about 3 minutes.

Turn the heat down to low and add the ginger, garlic, chile, ground cumin, coriander, and turmeric and sauté until the mixture smells aromatic, about 2 minutes. Take care not to let it burn. Add the tomato, cover, and cook until saucy, another 2 minutes.

Increase the heat to high and stir in the ground peas, the remaining ½ cup [120 ml] of water, and the salt and bring to a boil. Turn the heat down to a simmer, and cook for 1½ to 2 minutes, until the raw flavor disappears—you can taste to check this if you'd like. Just remember that peas don't take long to cook. Remove from the heat, stir in the lemon juice, adjust the salt as needed, and serve hot.

> **SERVING TIP:** I like to serve this over a bowl of plain steamed rice.

Fried Red Tomato Curry

(VE/GF)

¼ cup [60 ml] canola oil

1 tsp cumin seeds

10 to 15 curry leaves

2 Tbsp julienned ginger

2 Tbsp sliced garlic

2 tsp cayenne

½ tsp ground turmeric

2 lb [910 g] ripe red tomatoes, cut into ½ in [13 mm] thick rounds

1½ tsp ground coriander

1½ tsp sugar

1 tsp kosher salt, or more as needed

Goan lunches were always a bit heavy for me. Rice, curry, and fried fish in the middle of a sweltering day would make me want to head home and pass out. But I loved going out for breakfast; a light, spicy curry with crusty bread would start my day just right! There were all kinds of curries to choose from: mung beans, slow-cooked red or black-eyed peas, and my fave, tomat salaat—simply tomatoes and sliced onions cooked together with spices. Here I've done away with the onions and added curry leaves—with delicious results.

SERVES 4 TO 6

Heat the oil in a wok over medium heat until very hot. Add the cumin seeds and let them sputter. Immediately add the curry leaves, ginger, and garlic, stir, and move the wok off the heat. Add the cayenne, turmeric, and tomatoes and then return the wok to the heat. (Do this off the heat so the delicate turmeric and cayenne don't burn.)

Add the coriander, sugar, and salt, cover, and cook over medium-high heat for 5 to 6 minutes. You want about half of the tomatoes to break down but the rest should retain some shape. Serve warm. This will last in the refrigerator, tightly covered, for over a week.

> **SERVING TIP:** Make a little extra so you always have some in the refrigerator. It instantly elevates basic dishes! I like to serve this over toast garnished with coarsely chopped cilantro, tossed with pasta, or stirred into eggs.

Indian Pineapple Curry

(VE/GF)

1 tsp coriander seeds

2 Tbsp red lentils

1 Tbsp sesame or coconut oil

¼ tsp asafetida

½ tsp ground turmeric

½ tsp cayenne

14 oz [400 g] fresh pineapple, cut into 1 in [2.5 cm] pieces

1 tsp kosher salt

1 cup [240 ml] water

1 Tbsp fresh lemon juice (optional)

Pineapples were brought to India by the Portuguese in the 1500s (along with the cashew tree), and India is now one of the world's largest producers of pineapples. The spiky plants love the hot, humid climate. In Goa, I even used them as a fast-growing natural border to keep out the stray dogs who would wander into the garden to cool off in our fish pond. Pineapple curries are popular in Thailand and Sri Lanka, but my version has distinctly Indian flavors.

SERVES 4

Heat a cast-iron skillet over medium heat and toast the coriander seeds until lightly browned and fragrant, about 1 minute. Transfer to a bowl and set aside.

Add the lentils to the skillet and toast until lightly browned, 1 minute. Be careful not to burn them. Transfer the lentils to a spice grinder and allow to cool slightly. Pulse to coarsely grind and reserve.

Wipe down the skillet and reheat it over medium heat until hot. Add the oil, asafetida, turmeric, and then the cayenne. Quickly add the pineapple and salt and stir. Pour in the water and bring to a boil. Turn the heat down to a simmer, stir in the toasted coriander seeds and the ground lentils and mix well. Simmer for a few minutes, until the pineapple is cooked and some of it has turned pulpy. Taste the curry, and if the pineapple is too sweet, add the lemon juice to balance out the flavor. Serve warm.

> **SERVING TIP:** I like to serve this with batter-fried fish, potato fries, and a green salad.

Devil's Dung Potatoes

(VE option/GF/IP)

4 large russet potatoes

2 Tbsp ghee or canola oil

1 tsp cumin seeds

½ tsp asafetida

1 tsp ground turmeric

1 cup [240 ml] water

1 green chile, quartered lengthwise

1½ tsp kosher salt

I couldn't resist the name, because these saucy potatoes wouldn't be half as good without asafetida. A generous amount of the magical spice gives the dish its wonderful onion-garlic flavor, despite the fact that neither of those ingredients is present. For this reason, asafetida is also popular among certain Indian communities who avoid onion and garlic.

SERVES 4 TO 6

Place the potatoes in a pan with water to cover and bring to a boil over medium-high heat. Boil, covered, for 10 minutes. Remove from the heat and set aside, covered, for another 10 minutes. Drain the potatoes and wait until they're cool enough to handle. Peel and cut them into 1 in [2.5 cm] cubes.

Heat the ghee in a wok over medium heat and add the cumin seeds. When they're done sputtering, in quick succession add the asafetida, turmeric, and the cubed potatoes. Stir for a couple of minutes, allowing the potatoes to color a bit. Add ¼ cup [60 ml] of the water and deglaze the pan, scraping up any potatoes that have stuck to the bottom of the wok. Add the remaining ¾ cup [180 ml] of water, the chile, and salt and bring to a boil. Lower the heat to low, mash a few of the potato cubes—this thickens the curry a bit—and simmer, covered for about 5 minutes. Serve immediately.

INSTANT POT: First boil the potatoes in the Instant Pot. Place the potatoes with water to cover in the pot and Pressure Cook for 10 minutes. Quick-release the pressure and then cool, peel, and cut the potatoes. Wipe out the insert and use the Sauté function to proceed with the rest of the recipe.

SERVING TIP: I like to serve this with grilled coriander-and-turmeric-dusted tofu squares.

Monsoon Bamboo Curry

(VE/GF)

Young bamboo shoots are harvested during the rainy season in India. There are various ways to cook them, depending on the region. They are fermented in the northeastern states, pickled in South India, and sautéed and curried everywhere. Traditionally, cooking bamboo shoots is a bit of a slog; they have to be boiled and peeled before you can even get to the recipe. So I'm glad that you can get the shoots already prepared, in the refrigerated section of Asian grocers, or in cans in your local supermarket.

SERVES 4

COCONUT PASTE
1 tsp coconut oil

1 Tbsp coriander seeds

1 tsp cumin seeds

½ cup [40 g] dried, shredded, unsweetened coconut

½ cup [120 ml] water

One 8 oz [230 g] can bamboo shoots, drained (see Tip)

2 Tbsp coconut oil

½ tsp mustard seeds

¼ tsp asafetida

1 cup [140 g] finely chopped red onion

15 curry leaves

1 Tbsp sliced garlic

1 tsp cayenne

1½ cups [360 ml] water

1 tsp kosher salt

½ tsp sugar

1 Tbsp rice flour

½ cup [20 g] chopped cilantro leaves

To make the coconut paste: Place a cast-iron skillet over medium heat and add the 1 tsp oil, follow with the coriander and cumin seeds, then add the coconut. Stirring constantly, brown the seeds and coconut, 2 to 3 minutes. Take care not to burn the coconut. Transfer to a blender, add the water, and pulse until you have a smooth paste. Set aside.

If using whole bamboo shoots, cut into 1 in [2.5 cm] pieces.

Heat the 2 Tbsp oil in a wok over medium heat. When it starts smoking, add the mustard seeds. When they stop popping, add the asafetida, onion, and curry leaves. Brown the onion slightly, about 3 minutes. Add the garlic and cayenne and stir-fry for 1 minute.

Now add the coconut paste and simmer, uncovered, for 2 minutes, stirring often. Add the water to the blender, swirl it around to incorporate any remaining coconut paste, then add it to the wok. Mix well and bring to a boil. Add the bamboo shoots, salt, and sugar, turn the heat down to medium-low, and simmer for 4 minutes. Whisk in the rice flour and simmer for another 2 minutes. Mix in the cilantro. Serve hot or at room temperature.

TIP: Buy bamboo shoots whole or in slices, not the thin strips.

SERVING TIP: I like to serve this over soft rice noodles with a cucumber salad.

Alluring Asparagus

(VE/GF)

2 Tbsp mustard oil

½ tsp mustard seeds

¼ tsp asafetida

1 bunch (10½ oz [300 g]) asparagus, woody ends trimmed

1 tsp ground coriander

Sprinkle of sea salt

Lemon wedges, for serving

There's a popular Ayurvedic remedy made from a variety of asparagus that grows high up in the Himalayas. The name of the remedy is Shatavari, which translates as "she who possesses a hundred husbands." As the name suggests, it's often taken to enhance feminine health and libido. But even your common garden asparagus has a libidinous history, recommended hundreds of years ago in *The Perfumed Garden*, the Arabic equivalent of the *Kama Sutra*. While erotic claims make for a delicious story, I think asparagus just makes a delicious dish. Here, potent mustard oil gives it a tempting Indian twist.

SERVES 4

Heat a cast-iron skillet over high heat until very hot. Working quickly, add the oil to the super-heated skillet and then add the mustard seeds. When they're done sputtering—this will only take a few seconds—add the asafetida and, immediately after, add the asparagus.

Sear over high heat until all the spears have a nice char on them. Add the coriander, and using a pair of tongs, turn to coat with the spice and to evenly char the asparagus. Do not overcook. Transfer to a serving platter, sprinkle with salt, and serve with the lemon wedges.

> **SERVING TIP:** I like to serve this with lemon-garlic-butter-baked fish.

Cauliflower with Raisins

(VE option/GF)

¼ cup [35 g] black raisins

¼ cup [60 ml] apple cider vinegar

1 medium head cauliflower

1 large carrot

4 Tbsp ghee or canola oil

1 cup [140 g] finely chopped red onion

2 Tbsp grated ginger

1 tsp ground turmeric

1 tsp cayenne

1 cup [200 g] finely chopped tomatoes

2 tsp ground coriander

½ tsp ground cumin

¼ cup [10 g] chopped cilantro leaves

1 tsp kosher salt

1 tsp sugar

½ cup [120 ml] water

Let's be honest: Cauliflower can be bland. That absence of flavor is why it does well in its new avatars of cauliflower rice and pizza crust: as a neutral backdrop for the actual dish. In *5 Spices, 50 Dishes*, I went the opposite direction and made the vegetable fancy, steaming a whole cauliflower and making an aromatic sauce to pour over. Here I've kept it weeknight-friendly but added carrots and vinegar-plumped raisins for an extra bit of pizazz.

SERVES 4 TO 6

Soak the raisins in the vinegar, and set aside while you prep the other ingredients. It'll take about 30 minutes for the raisins to plump up.

Cut the cauliflower into 1 in [2.5 cm] florets. Peel the carrot, halve lengthwise, and then chop crosswise into ½ in [13 mm] half-moons. Heat about half of the ghee in a wok over medium heat and fry the cauliflower florets and carrot pieces together until browned all over, about 5 minutes. Remove and set aside.

Add the remaining ghee to the wok and cook the onion until brown, about 4 minutes. Add the ginger, turmeric, and cayenne and sauté for 2 minutes. Now mix in the tomatoes, coriander, and cumin and cook, covered, for 2 minutes more or until saucy.

Uncover and add the soaked raisins, including any remaining vinegar, the cilantro, salt, sugar, and the fried cauliflower and carrot. Toss well. Add the water, mix well, cover, and cook until the vegetables are crisp-tender, 3 to 4 minutes. Serve warm.

SERVING TIP: I like to serve this with seared lamb chops.

Holy Mushroom Curry

(VE/GF)

1 cup [80 g] dried, shredded, unsweetened coconut

3 Tbsp canola oil

2 cups [280 g] finely chopped red onions

1 Tbsp minced garlic

1 tsp cayenne

1 tsp ground coriander

½ tsp ground turmeric

½ tsp ground cumin

1 cup [240 ml] water

8 oz [230 g] button mushrooms

2 tsp kosher salt

As the July thunderstorms turn to steady rain in August, all that Goans can talk about are olmi. These elusive wild mushrooms grow in the forest on sacred termite mounds, and the locations are kept secret by local villagers. The forager must appease the guardian snake of the termite mound by offering a wild herb called akshar. Only then can she pick the delicate olmi, being careful to leave half of the fungi behind. No wonder these mushrooms command a handsome price; a small bundle wrapped in a large leaf can cost as much as two days' wages. Since we have no sacred termite mounds here in the West, we'll substitute the humble button mushroom to make this well-known Goan mushroom dish.

SERVES 4

Heat a cast-iron skillet over medium heat. Once warm, add the coconut to toast, 3 to 4 minutes. When it is lightly browned, scrape into a bowl. Wipe out the skillet with a paper towel and return to the heat.

Add 1 Tbsp of the oil and 1 cup [140 g] of the onions to the hot skillet and brown well, about 5 minutes. Add the garlic, cayenne, coriander, turmeric, and cumin and stir for 1 minute more. Transfer the spiced onions to a blender jar, add the reserved coconut, and pulse a couple of times to mix everything up. Now slowly add the water, drizzling in a little at a time to make a smooth paste. Stop and scrape down the sides of the jar multiple times to ensure it's well mixed.

Quarter the larger mushrooms, halve the medium ones, and keep any little ones whole—you want 1 in [2.5 cm] pieces.

Heat the remaining 2 Tbsp of oil in the wok over medium heat and fry the remaining 1 cup [140 g] of chopped onions until golden brown. Add the mushrooms and sauté until they soften slightly. Add the salt and the coconut paste and mix well. Cook for 5 minutes or until the mushrooms have softened, stirring often.

SERVING TIP: I like to serve this with roasted baby red potatoes, a green salad, and crusty bread.

CHAPTER

4

Hearty Dals and Beans

There is nothing so quintessentially Indian as *dal-chawal*, or dal and rice, the comfort food of princes and paupers. There's also nothing so confusing: Are we talking about lentils, legumes, beans? Technically, dals are split versions of pulses, a group that includes dry lentils, cowpeas, and pigeon peas, and beans like garbanzo and mung. You split mung beans, you get mung dal. But then, a stew made with *any* kind of pulse—whole or split—is also called a dal. I told you it was confusing. So why try to understand dal when it's so much easier to just cook it? Use one of my recipes and your Instant Pot to make a delicious dal that's also a fantastic source of protein and fiber.

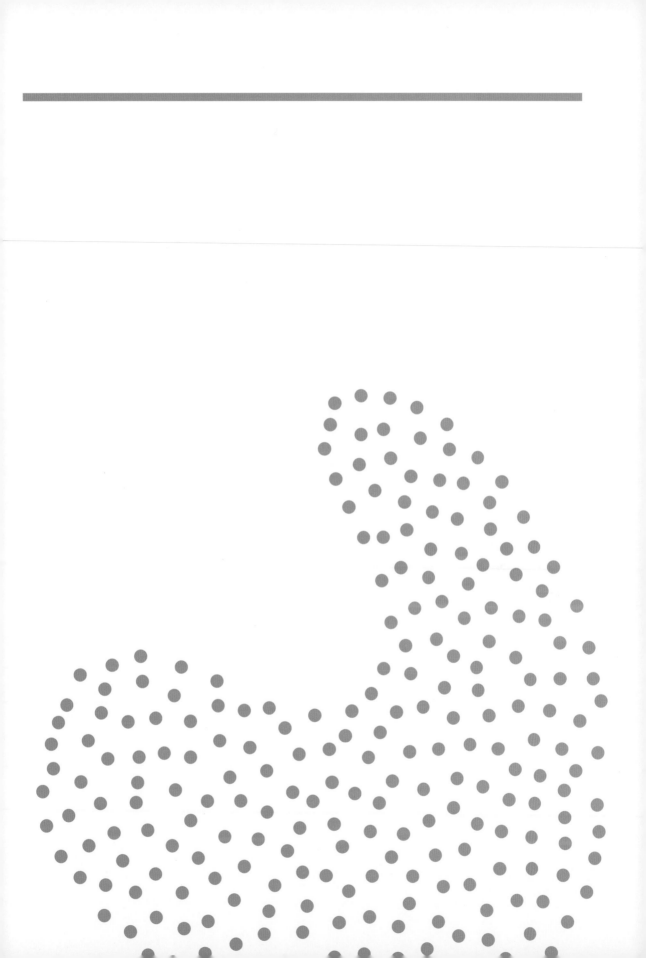

Parsi-Style Rajma

(VE/GF)

3 Tbsp canola oil

1 cup [140 g] finely chopped yellow onion

1 Tbsp grated ginger

1 Tbsp grated garlic

1 Tbsp ground coriander

1½ tsp cayenne

1 tsp ground turmeric

1 tsp ground cumin

1 cup [200 g] finely chopped tomatoes

One 16 oz [455 g] can red kidney beans

1 cup [240 ml] water

2 Tbsp brown sugar

2 tsp kosher salt

½ cup [120 ml] coconut milk

Red kidney beans, or rajma, are generally associated with the Punjabi preparation served over rice in countless northern Indian homes. But in this recipe, I take my cues from the Parsi community, who use coconut milk to finish off the dish. For a further hint of sweetness, they add jaggery; I use the more commonly available brown sugar. By the way, this dish tastes even better once it "blooms" after a few hours, making it a perfect choice for a dinner party. Or make a double batch on the weekend and enjoy several meals during the week.

SERVES 4

In a wok over medium heat, warm the oil. Add the onion and sauté until golden brown, about 5 minutes. Add the ginger, garlic, coriander, cayenne, turmeric, and cumin. Lower the heat to medium and sauté the mixture until it smells fragrant.

Add the tomatoes, cover, and cook until it all turns saucy and thickens slightly, 5 to 6 minutes. Add the red beans, water, sugar, and salt and stir well. Bring to a boil, then turn the heat down to low, and simmer for 3 to 4 minutes, until creamy and thickened slightly.

Add the coconut milk and heat through, about 2 minutes. Serve warm.

> **SERVING TIP:** I like to serve this with steamed basmati rice, onions pickled in red wine vinegar, and a whole green chile!

Hill Country Beans

(GF/IP)

Two 14 oz [400 g] cans black soybeans (see Tip)

1½ cups [360 ml] water, or more if needed

½ cup [70 g] finely chopped red onion

2 Tbsp minced garlic

2 Tbsp minced ginger

1 tsp ground coriander

1 tsp ground cumin

½ tsp ground turmeric

½ tsp cayenne

2 Tbsp canola oil

2 green chiles, quartered lengthwise

1 tsp kosher salt

2 Tbsp ghee

1 tsp cumin seeds

¼ tsp asafetida

Black soybeans are a nutritious and hearty staple in the Himalayan state of Uttarakhand, where winters are severe and the hardy people of the hills eat simple, rib-sticking foods. This dish is traditionally made in an iron kadai, or wok, which lends the curry a rich, dark hue. After soaking overnight, the beans are coarsely ground, then stirred into a fragrant sauce and simmered for hours.

SERVES 4 TO 6

Using a blender, pulse the beans until coarsely ground. You can use up to 1 cup [240 ml] of the water to help the blades along. Remove the ground beans to a bowl and rinse out the blender.

Add the onion, garlic, ginger, coriander, ground cumin, turmeric, and cayenne to the blender and purée until smooth, adding a little water if required.

Heat the oil in a wok and add the onion-spice paste. Sauté over low heat, until your kitchen smells maddeningly aromatic. Add in the ground soybeans, chiles, the remaining ½ cup [120 ml] of water, and the salt. Stir well, bring to a boil, and then turn down to a simmer for about 15 minutes. Simmering really deepens the flavor of this dish.

To finish the dish, heat the ghee in a small skillet, and when it starts smoking, add the cumin seeds. When the seeds are done sputtering, add the asafetida and immediately pour over the cooked beans. Serve hot.

INSTANT POT: Follow the instructions through sautéing the onion-spice paste. Add the coarsely ground soybeans, the sautéed onion mixture, chiles, ½ cup [120 ml] water, and the salt to the Instant Pot. Cook on the Stew setting for 10 minutes. Let the pressure release naturally and finish off the dish with the hot spiced ghee. You could even use the Delay Start feature, putting everything into the pot in the morning to have it ready for you by dinnertime.

> **TIP:** If you can't find black soybeans, use regular soybeans or even regular black beans.

> **SERVING TIP:** I like to serve this as a stew with the Mustard and Cilantro Greens with Burnt Onions (page 69).

Spicy Curried Mung Sprouts

(VE option/GF)

I always have sprouts in my refrigerator; they're a great last-minute addition to salads or sandwiches. I sprout all kinds of things, but mung beans are my favorite because of how quickly they sprout. Some beans and grains take so long to germinate that harmful bacteria can grow alongside. That's why you're supposed to lightly steam your sprouts before eating them. Here's a great way to enjoy your sprouts—serve with crusty bread rolls, or simply crumble potato chips on top for extra crunch.

SERVES 4

1 cup [200 g] whole green mung beans

CURRY
2 Tbsp ghee or canola oil

1 tsp mustard seeds

½ tsp cumin seeds

½ tsp ground turmeric

¼ tsp asafetida

1 Tbsp ground coriander

1 tsp cayenne

1 tsp ground cumin

3 cups [710 ml] water

1 Tbsp brown sugar

2 tsp kosher salt

RELISH
½ cup [70 g] finely chopped red onion

¼ cup [50 g] finely chopped tomato

¼ cup [10 g] chopped cilantro leaves

2 Tbsp fresh lemon juice, or more as needed

1 Tbsp minced green chile

1 tsp Himalayan pink salt, or more as needed

Potato chips, crumbled, for garnish

Rinse the mung beans in a couple of changes of water and then place in a bowl and cover with plenty of water. Let soak overnight or for 6 to 8 hours. Drain the water out and discard any beans that haven't plumped up: You will easily hear them rattling noisily in your bowl. Now transfer the soaked mung beans to a glass container and loosely cover with a lid; you want to ensure that air can still reach the beans. Set aside in a dark corner of the kitchen—the beans should sprout in a day. At this point you can proceed with the recipe or transfer the sprouts to the refrigerator in an airtight container where they will keep for a week.

To make the curry: Heat the ghee in a wok over medium heat. When it's hot, add the mustard and cumin seeds. When they've stopped popping, add the turmeric and asafetida and then the sprouted mung beans. Follow with the coriander, cayenne, and ground cumin and toss well. Add the water, sugar, and kosher salt and bring to a boil. Turn down the heat to low, cover, and simmer until the sprouts are cooked and the sauce has reduced a little bit, 10 to 12 minutes.

To make the relish: In a small bowl, mix together the onion, tomato, cilantro, lemon juice, chile, and pink salt. Taste for salt and tartness and adjust to your liking.

To serve, ladle out some of the hot curry in a bowl, and then top with the relish and some crumbled potato chips.

> **SERVING TIP:** I like to serve this with just some crusty bread for dipping.

Fasting Curry (GF)

1 cup [140 g] shelled, unroasted peanuts

1 green chile, seeded

1 Tbsp minced ginger

¼ tsp ground turmeric

1 cup [240 g] plain whole-milk or low-fat yogurt

3 cups [710 ml] water

2 tsp Himalayan pink salt

2 Tbsp ghee

1 tsp cumin seeds

¼ tsp cayenne

Growing up in India, I snacked on a lot of peanuts: roasted and spiced at the street food vendor; freshly pulled out of the earth as a muddy snack; boiled in their shells as a more civilized one. Peanuts are also regularly cooked into Indian veggie stir-fries and curries.

Many Hindus fast intermittently, particularly during religious festivals. Religion aside, these fasts are often based on the season, and the end goal is to maintain a balanced and healthy constitution. Certain foods—including peanuts—are acceptable during fasting, as they help cleanse and detoxify the body, while also providing much-needed energy during lean meal times. You're cooking yogurt—it doesn't seem intuitive, and you're right, you will have a curdled mess on your hands if you're not careful. Just don't let the curry boil and you'll be fine. The ground peanuts help stabilize the yogurt, and as long as you watch your pot, all will go well.

SERVES 4

Soak the peanuts in water to cover for 2 hours. Drain and add to a blender jar along with the chile, ginger, and turmeric and blitz to chop as finely as you can. Next add the yogurt and purée until smooth. Then add 1 cup [240 ml] of the water and use the highest setting to blend together well.

Transfer the mixture to a wok and stir in the remaining 2 cups [475 ml] of water and the salt. Place the wok over medium heat and bring to a simmer gently, stirring all the while.

Simmer, stirring often, until the peanuts are cooked and the curry has thickened a bit, 6 to 8 minutes.

Meanwhile, heat the ghee in a small skillet over medium heat. When it starts smoking, add the cumin seeds. When the seeds are done sputtering, add the cayenne and immediately pour the spiced oil over the simmering curry. Remove from the heat and serve hot.

SERVING TIP: I like to serve this as a soup or over Fluffy Millet with Cashews (page 123).

Split Peas with Zucchini and Green Beans

(VE option/GF/IP)

⅓ cup [65 g] split peas

3 cups [710 ml] water

1½ tsp kosher salt

½ tsp asafetida

¾ tsp ground turmeric

2 Tbsp ghee or canola oil

½ tsp mustard seeds

½ tsp cumin seeds

1 medium zucchini,
cut into 1 in [2.5 cm] pieces

4 oz [115 g] green beans,
cut into 1 in [2.5 cm] lengths

1 Tbsp ground coriander

1 tsp cayenne

½ cup [120 ml] coconut milk

Split peas have a grassy flavor that makes me feel close to the earth. We'll prepare this dish in three parts: First, we'll use turmeric and asafetida to break down the gas in the peas. Then we'll use asafetida once more, this time for flavor, by adding it to the hot oil for the zucchini. Finally, we'll combine the split peas and zucchini, both perfectly cooked. Keeping them separate until the end ensures that the zucchini doesn't get overcooked.

SERVES 4

Rinse and soak the split peas in water to cover for at least 30 minutes and up to overnight. If you're using an Instant Pot, you can skip this step (see note).

Drain the peas and add to a medium stockpot. Top with 2½ cups [600 ml] of the water, 1 tsp of the salt, ¼ tsp of the asafetida, and ¼ tsp of the turmeric and bring to a boil. Cover, lower the heat to low, and simmer until the peas are tender, about 20 minutes.

Heat the ghee in a wok and when it is smoking add the mustard and cumin seeds. When they're done sputtering, in quick succession add the remaining ¼ tsp of asafetida, the remaining ½ tsp of turmeric, the zucchini, and the green beans. Add the coriander, cayenne, and the remaining ½ tsp of salt and toss well. Cover and cook until the vegetables are just barely tender and still hold their shape, 2 to 3 minutes.

Transfer the vegetables to the stockpot, scraping up the flavorful spices and ghee.

In a small bowl, whisk the coconut milk with the remaining ½ cup [120 ml] of water and add it to the stockpot. Stir gently and bring back up to a simmer. Let simmer for an additional 3 minutes to allow the flavors to meld, but do not overcook. Serve hot.

INSTANT POT: Rinse and drain the split peas and add them to the Instant Pot. Add 2 cups [475 ml] of the water and Pressure Cook on High for 10 minutes. Then quick-release the pressure and proceed with the rest of the recipe. Cook the vegetables in a wok and transfer them to the Instant Pot. Turn the Sauté function on High and continue with the coconut milk, simmering for 3 minutes to combine all the flavors well.

> **SERVING TIP:** I like to serve this with fluffy quinoa cooked with raisins and almonds.

Sour Mango Dal

(VE option/GF/IP)

½ cup [100 g] pink lentils

3 cups [710 ml] water

1 cup [140 g] chopped mango (½ in [13 mm] dice)

½ cup [100 g] finely chopped ripe tomato

1 Tbsp minced ginger

1 Tbsp minced green chile

1 tsp ground turmeric

2 Tbsp ghee or canola oil

½ tsp mustard seeds

½ tsp cumin seeds

½ tsp asafetida

1 tsp cayenne

1 tsp ground coriander

1 tsp kosher salt

1 tsp sugar

¼ cup [10 g] chopped cilantro leaves

1 Tbsp fresh lemon juice

Ghee, melted, for drizzling (optional)

Many Indian recipes have tart flavors, sourness being one of the six tastes recommended by Ayurveda for a balanced diet. While lime or lemon juice automatically come to mind, Indians have several other subtle souring agents at their disposal: yogurt, tamarind, and a range of sour fruits like raw mango, kokum (a variety of mangosteen), and ambade, the Indian hog plum. This dal uses unripe mango to add some tartness.

SERVES 4

Rinse the lentils and place in a stockpot with 2 cups [475 ml] of the water, ½ cup [70 g] of the mango, the tomato, ginger, chile, and ½ tsp of the turmeric. Bring to a boil. Turn down the heat to medium-low and simmer, covered, until the lentils are mushy, about 10 minutes.

Heat the ghee in a small skillet, and when it starts smoking, add the mustard and cumin seeds. When they stop sputtering, add the asafetida, the remaining ½ tsp of turmeric, and the cayenne. Stir quickly and immediately pour the spiced ghee over the mushy lentils. Add the remaining 1 cup [240 ml] of water, the remaining ½ cup [70 g] of mango, the coriander, salt, and sugar to the dal and stir well. At this point you can add more water if you prefer your dal to be a little thinner. Simmer the dal for 4 to 5 minutes, until the freshly added mango is tender but still holds its shape. Mix in the cilantro and lemon juice. Serve hot, with ghee to drizzle on top.

INSTANT POT: Rinse the lentils and add to the Instant Pot with only 1 cup [240 ml] of the water, ½ cup [70 g] of the mango, the tomato, ginger, chile, and ½ tsp of the turmeric. Pressure Cook on High for 5 minutes. Quick-release the pressure and proceed with the rest of the recipe.

> **SERVING TIP:** I like to serve this with the Roasted Eggs with Fennel (page 136) and basmati rice.

Pink Lentils with Kale

(VE option/GF/IP)

1 cup [200 g] pink lentils, rinsed

½ cup [100 g] chopped tomato

2 Tbsp minced ginger

1 tsp kosher salt

½ tsp ground turmeric

3½ cups [830 ml] water

1 bunch (7 oz [200 g]) curly kale, thinly sliced (see Tip)

2 green chiles, quartered lengthwise

2 Tbsp ghee or canola oil

1 tsp cumin seeds

¼ tsp asafetida

I'm forever trying to sneak vegetables into everything! Veggies combined with a meat dish, greens in a dal, sprouts in a sandwich—it's a simple way to get a fair number of vegetables into my family every day. Here's a great way to veget-ize a dal with hearty kale. While some people use spinach in a similar fashion, it's delicate and dissolves too quickly for my taste.

SERVES 4

Place the rinsed lentils, tomato, ginger, salt, turmeric, and 2½ cups [600 ml] of the water in a saucepan and bring to a boil. Turn the heat down, cover, and simmer until the lentils are mushy, about 10 minutes. Stir in the kale, the remaining 1 cup [240 ml] of water, and the chiles and continue simmering for another 5 minutes, until the kale is wilted.

Heat the ghee in a small skillet over high heat, and when it starts smoking, add the cumin seeds. When the seeds are done sputtering, add the asafetida and immediately pour over the lentils. Serve hot.

INSTANT POT: Add the rinsed lentils, tomato, ginger, salt, turmeric, and only 1½ cups [360 ml] of water to the Instant Pot. Cook on High Pressure for 10 minutes. Quick-release the pressure and open the cooker. Turn on the Sauté setting and stir in the kale, 1 cup [240 ml] of water, and the chiles and simmer for 5 minutes. Finish off the dish with the hot spiced ghee.

> **TIP:** Don't use lacinato kale; the leaves are way too thick. The curly kind does the job perfectly. To prepare the kale, cut off the bottom third or the fibrous part of the stems, retaining the more tender stalks. Roll up the leaves and slice crosswise thinly.

> **SERVING TIP:** I like to serve this with steamed rice, Spicy Red Pickled Chicken (page 148), and Avocado Raita (page 53).

CHAPTER

5

Nourishing Grains and More

You may be surprised to find very little wheat or rice in this section. Growing up, we ate many other interesting grains, and I wanted to showcase some of them here. Indian farmer grains like barley, sorghum, and amaranth all appeared regularly at our dinner table. My mother, ever the experimental cook, would grind them into flour to make flatbreads, pancakes, and fritters, or cook them whole into fluffy pilafs. While technically not grains, mung beans and chickpeas also appear here as wonderful gluten-free substitutes for wheat.

I'm so excited that many of these ingredients, bursting with nutrition and flavor, are now widely available. And I hope these recipes will help introduce some of them to your own kitchen.

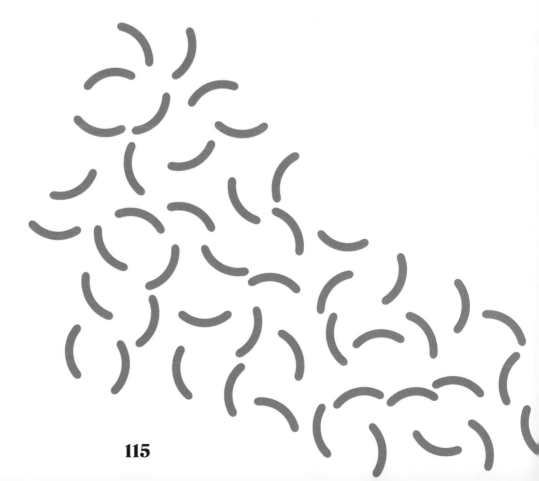

Spiced Oat Pancakes

(GF option)

1 cup [120 g] oat flour

½ cup [80 g] semolina or coarsely ground rice flour

2 Tbsp dried, shredded, unsweetened coconut

½ tsp cumin seeds

1½ cups [360 ml] water

½ cup [120 g] plain whole-milk or low-fat yogurt

1 tsp kosher salt

¾ cup [150 g] finely chopped tomatoes

½ cup [24 g] finely chopped green onions, white and green parts

1 Tbsp minced green chile

2 Tbsp canola oil or ghee

Uttapa are delicious South Indian pancakes, eaten at breakfast or as a snack. They're usually made with a rice and dal batter, but I've found that semolina delivers better texture and mouthfeel, and oat flour dials up the nutrition. Want to keep it gluten-free? My recipe gives you the option of using coarsely ground rice flour instead of semolina. Can't find the coarse grind? It's so easy to make your own using a spice grinder. Just measure out the rice and pulse until coarsely ground.

MAKES 6 PANCAKES

In a medium bowl, stir the oat flour, semolina, and coconut together. Crush the cumin seeds by rubbing them between your palms—this releases their aromatic oils—and add to the flour mix.

In a separate medium bowl, whisk 1 cup [240 ml] of the water, the yogurt, and salt together. Add to the flour mix, then stir in the tomatoes, green onions, and chile. Set aside for 10 minutes, or even overnight, covered in the refrigerator.

When you're ready to make the pancakes, place a cast-iron skillet over medium heat. To test if it's hot enough, sprinkle a little water on the surface of the skillet—it should almost instantly sizzle off. Brush a little oil or ghee on the skillet.

The batter may thicken as it sits; if it's too thick, stir in the remaining ½ cup [120 ml] of water. We want it to be of a pouring consistency. Using a ½ cup [120 ml] ladle, pour the batter in the center of the skillet. Either swirl the pan to spread the batter or use the back of the ladle to make a larger circle of the batter. Cover and cook until the edges start to look brown, about 1 minute.

Uncover and drizzle a little oil or ghee along the edges of the pancake and then flip it. Cook the other side, 30 to 45 seconds, until lightly browned. Transfer the pancake to a plate and repeat with the rest of the batter. These savory pancakes are delightful on their own and don't need any accompaniment. While best eaten straight from the skillet, they keep pretty well too. Just refrigerate in a covered container, and reheat on a hot skillet.

Mung Bean and Cottage Cheese Wraps (GF)

FILLING

1¼ cups [350g] cottage cheese

¼ cup [35 g] finely chopped green onions, both white and green parts

¼ tsp ground cumin

¼ tsp cayenne

Sprinkle of salt

CRÊPES

1 cup [200 g] whole green mung beans

One 2½ in [6 cm] piece ginger

1 cup [240 ml] water

2 tsp kosher salt, or more as needed

1 tsp sesame seeds

¼ tsp ground turmeric

1 tsp cumin seeds

½ cup [70 g] finely chopped red onion

1 Tbsp minced green chile

Up to ¼ cup [60 ml] sesame oil

By now you can probably tell how much I love mung beans! I've got three mung bean recipes in this cookbook—all different—which also proves how versatile these little beans are. Here we'll grind them to make a batter for a savory pancake. They're delicious just like that, but I'll kick it up a notch by stuffing the pancakes with spiced cottage cheese. And if I want to go all out, I might add some arugula and maybe a slice or two of avocado on top of the cottage cheese.

MAKES 10 WRAPS

To make the filling: In a medium bowl, gently mix the cottage cheese, green onions, ground cumin, and cayenne together. Season with salt.

To make the crêpes: Rinse the mung beans in a couple of changes of water, place in a bowl, and cover with plenty of water. Let soak overnight or for 6 to 8 hours. Drain the water and discard any beans that haven't plumped up. You can easily identify them—they're the ones rattling noisily in the bottom of your bowl.

In a blender jar, first place the ginger and pulse to chop it up as finely as you can. Then add the soaked mung beans and pulse briefly. With the blender running, add the water in a slow stream through the lid to purée the beans to a smooth paste. Transfer to a bowl and add the salt, sesame seeds, and turmeric. Crush the cumin seeds by rubbing them between your palms—this releases their aromatic oils—before adding to the puréed beans. Stir in the red onion and chile and taste for salt.

Place a cast-iron skillet over medium-high heat and test if it's hot enough by sprinkling a little water on it. If the drops of water immediately sizzle off, then you're ready to proceed. Brush a little oil on the skillet. Using a ½ cup [120 ml] ladle, pour the batter in the center of the skillet. Using the back of the ladle, spread the batter in a circular motion to make a 6 in [15 cm] circle. Cover and cook until the edges start to look brown, about 1 minute. Uncover and drizzle with a little oil along the edges of the crêpe and then flip it. Repeat with the remaining batter.

To serve, place 2 Tbsp of the filling in the middle of each crêpe. Fold one side of the crêpe over the filling and then wrap the other side on top. Secure with a toothpick if you'd like.

Chickpea Crêpes with Shishito Peppers

(VE/GF)

4 Tbsp peanut oil

18 shishito peppers
(4½ oz [130 g])

2 tsp kosher salt

½ Tbsp fresh lemon juice

1 medium zucchini, thinly
sliced into half-moons

1 tsp dried Mexican
oregano, crumbled

1 cup [120 g] chana besan or
chickpea flour

¼ tsp asafetida

¼ tsp ground turmeric

¼ tsp cayenne

¼ tsp cumin seeds

1 cup [240 ml] water

Why is there oregano in this Indian recipe? First, because you probably already have it, and second, because I'm trying to approximate the flavor of the actual herb I'd like to use in this crêpe: Indian borage. Prized for its medicinal value, it grows within reach of every Goan kitchen. It's commonly used in herbal teas, but I've also used it to flavor soups and salad dressings. Indian borage has a flavor and aroma similar to Mexican oregano, which is why it's also known as Mexican mint.

MAKES 6 CRÊPES

Heat a cast-iron skillet over high heat until smoking, add 1 Tbsp of the oil, and throw in the peppers. Char one side and then, using tongs, flip them over so they get a nice char on the other side too. Sprinkle with 1 tsp of the salt and the lemon juice, toss, and transfer to a plate.

Reheat the skillet over high heat and add another 1 Tbsp of oil. Sear the zucchini until browned and slightly softened. Add the oregano and ½ tsp of the salt, mix together, and transfer to a medium bowl.

In a medium bowl, stir the chana besan with the asafetida, turmeric, cayenne, cumin seeds, and the remaining ½ tsp salt. Add the water and whisk to make a smooth batter.

Wipe out the skillet and return it to medium heat. Using ½ tsp oil per crêpe, brush it on the skillet and pour in ½ cup [120 ml] of batter. Immediately swirl the pan so the crêpe spreads into a thin 8 or 9 in [20 to 23 cm] circle. Drizzle another ½ tsp of oil along the circumference of the crêpe. Cook until bubbles form on the surface and the crêpe is golden brown on the underside, 30 to 40 seconds. Flip to briefly cook on the other side, no more than 30 seconds, and flip it back to its original side. Arrange one-sixth of the zucchini on one half of the crêpe. Top with three shishito peppers. Fold the crêpe over and serve hot. Make the remaining 5 crepes the same way.

Rice and Cucumber Crêpes

(VE/GF)

1 cup [140 g] rice flour

½ tsp kosher salt, or more as needed

¼ tsp cumin seeds

1 tsp sesame seeds

¼ tsp ground turmeric

1½ cups [360 ml] water

¾ cup [180 g] grated cucumber (use the large holes of a box grater)

½ tsp minced garlic

3 Tbsp sesame oil

Everybody loves dosas. But dosa batter takes forever to make—soak rice and dal for hours, grind each ingredient separately to a different consistency, set aside to ferment overnight or longer. These crêpes are my everyday answer to dosas. They are every bit as delicious, with a nice crunch from the cucumber, and I can have them ready minutes after the craving hits!

MAKES 6 TO 8 CRÊPES

In a medium bowl, stir the rice flour and salt together. Crush the cumin seeds by rubbing them between your palms—this releases their aromatic oils. Whisk the sesame seeds, cumin seeds, and turmeric into the flour. Stir in the water, cucumber, and garlic and combine well.

Heat a cast-iron skillet over medium-high heat and add 1 tsp of the oil. Using a ¼ cup [60 ml] ladle, pour the crêpe batter into the center of the pan. It'll spread out on its own, no need to tilt the pan. When little air bubbles form and the crêpe looks browned around the edges, about 2 minutes, lift one side to check underneath. If it looks golden brown, flip the crêpe, and cook the other side until golden brown as well. Serve warm. These are great as is, or see the serving tip.

These crêpes can be made ahead and kept refrigerated in an airtight container. To serve, just warm slightly in the microwave or on a hot skillet.

> **SERVING TIP:** I like to serve these with fried eggs and breakfast sausages.

Fluffy Millet with Cashews

(VE option/GF/IP)

1 Tbsp ghee or canola oil

½ tsp cumin seeds

1 cup [180 g] whole millet

½ cup [70 g] chopped carrot (¼ in [6 mm] dice)

¼ cup [35 g] toasted cashews

2 cups [475 ml] boiling water

1 tsp kosher salt

1 Tbsp fresh lemon juice

The word *millet* refers to a group of grasses that have been eaten for hundreds of years—hence the term *ancient grains*. Many varieties are grown in India, and now in the United States as well. Before wheat and rice took over Indian diets in the 1960s, millets were the daily grains of Indians, and I'm happy to see them making a bit of a comeback. Many millet varieties—pearl, finger, foxtail, and kodo—can be used interchangeably. I often serve millet instead of rice, and this recipe will let you do the same. In fact, omit the carrots and cashews, and you may fool your guests into thinking you've served a very small-grained rice.

SERVES 4

In a wok, heat the ghee over medium heat until smoking. Add the cumin seeds, and just as soon as they're done sputtering, throw in the millet. Stir constantly for 2 minutes, until toasty. Add the carrot and cashews and mix well.

Pour in the water and salt, stir, and bring to a boil. Turn the heat down to low, cover, and cook for 20 minutes. Remove from the heat and leave covered for another 5 minutes. Uncover, drizzle with the lemon juice, and fluff with a fork.

INSTANT POT: Add the ghee to the Instant Pot and turn the Sauté function on High. When the ghee is very hot, add the cumin seeds, and just as soon as they're done sputtering, throw in the millet. Stir constantly until toasty; it'll take about 4 minutes in the Instant Pot. Proceed with the rest of the recipe, using only 1½ cups [360 ml] of water. Use the manual Pressure Cook setting on High for 15 minutes. Let the pressure release naturally.

> **SERVING TIP:** I like to serve this with the Fasting Curry (page 104). This is also a great accompaniment to a Moroccan chickpea stew or served alongside a ratatouille.

Sorghum Pilaf with Purple Cauliflower

(VE/GF/IP)

1 cup [180 g] whole sorghum

6 cups [1.4 L] water

1½ tsp kosher salt

½ tsp ground turmeric

½ head purple cauliflower

1 medium carrot

4 large leaves of kale, collard greens, or cauliflower

2 Tbsp peanut oil

1 tsp mustard seeds

¼ tsp asafetida

1 cup [140 g] chopped yellow onion

2 Tbsp minced ginger

1 Tbsp minced green chile

2 Tbsp fresh lemon juice

Jowar, or sorghum, is a millet that's usually ground into flour to make flatbreads in India. But as a whole grain, it makes an excellent salad; it has a satisfying farro-like chew, and when combined with vegetables, you get a nutrient-dense meal.

SERVES 4 TO 6

Rinse the sorghum, add water to cover, and soak for 8 hours. Drain and place in a stockpot. Add the water, ½ tsp of the salt, and ¼ tsp of the turmeric and bring to a boil. Turn the heat down to a simmer, cover, and cook until the grain is tender, about 30 minutes. Drain any excess water.

Cut the cauliflower into ¼ in [6 mm] florets and the carrot into ¼ in [6 mm] pieces. Stack the leaves and cut lengthwise into two, then roll into a cylinder and slice crosswise thinly.

Heat the oil in a wok over medium heat. When the oil just begins to smoke, add the mustard seeds. When they're done sputtering, add the asafetida, the remaining ¼ tsp turmeric, and then the onion, ginger, and chile. Sauté until the onion has colored slightly, 3 to 4 minutes. Add the cauliflower, carrot, greens, and ½ tsp of the salt, cover, and steam until the vegetables are crisp-tender but still retain their bright colors, about 3 minutes.

Add the cooked sorghum, the remaining ½ tsp of salt, and the lemon juice and mix gently but thoroughly. This can be served hot, cold, or at room temperature. You can also store it in a tightly covered container in the refrigerator for 4 to 5 days.

INSTANT POT: You can skip soaking the sorghum if you're using an Instant Pot. Rinse the sorghum and add 3 cups [710 ml] of water, ½ tsp of the salt, and ¼ tsp of the turmeric to the Instant Pot. Close the pot and set on the manual Pressure Cook setting on High for 30 minutes. Quick-release the pressure, drain any excess water, and proceed with the rest of the recipe.

> **SERVING TIP:** I like to serve this with classic meatballs in tomato sauce.

Aromatic Shrimp Pilaf

(GF/IP)

1½ cups [300 g] basmati rice

1 cup [20 g] cilantro leaves and tender stems, tightly packed

2 Tbsp minced garlic

1 Tbsp minced ginger

1 Tbsp minced green chile

½ tsp ground turmeric

2 Tbsp water, plus 2½ cups [600 ml]

3 Tbsp ghee or canola oil

1 cup [140 g] finely chopped red onion

8 oz [230 g] small shrimp, peeled and deveined

1½ tsp kosher salt

This recipe uses small shrimp, which will harden a bit as they cook along with the rice, imparting a nice briny flavor to your pilaf. If you can't find small enough shrimp, cut medium shrimp into two or three pieces using a pair of kitchen scissors.

SERVES 4 TO 6

Rinse the rice with two or three changes of water or until the water runs clear. Drain well.

In a blender, purée the cilantro, garlic, ginger, chile, turmeric, and the 2 Tbsp of water.

Heat the ghee in a large stockpot and sauté the onion until softened, 3 to 4 minutes. Add the cilantro purée and sauté well until very aromatic, 5 to 6 minutes. Add the shrimp, rice, and salt and mix well. Swirl the remaining 2½ cups [600 ml] of water into the blender and pour into the rice. Bring to a boil, lower the heat to low, and cook, covered, until tender, 10 minutes. Fluff the pilaf with a fork and serve hot.

INSTANT POT: Use the Sauté function to brown the onion and the cilantro purée. Press Cancel and continue with the recipe. Once the rice and shrimp are added, combine with only 2 cups [475 ml] of water. Use the Rice setting and cook for 7 minutes. Let the pressure release for 10 minutes naturally, then quick-release any remaining pressure.

> **SERVING TIP:** I like to serve this with any of the raitas in this book (pages 52–56) and a mesclun salad with goat cheese.

CHAPTER

6

Uncommon Mains: Eggs, Seafood, and Meat

I grew up mostly vegetarian, and I'm still a grazer at my core. But I understand carnivores because I live with one. My husband, Neville, is from a Goan Catholic background; his community considers it "fasting" if there's no beef or pork on the table. In coastal Goa, seafood is eaten daily. And during the monsoons, when fishing boats stay out of the choppy seas, Goans simply switch to dried fish. After thirty years of marriage, Neville has sort of adjusted to a mostly vegetarian diet at home. In fact, he can go three full meatless days before feeling "weak," as he puts it. Then it's time to roast a chicken, fry some pork, or make a fish curry.

Here are some "non-vegetarian" favorites from our home kitchen—although I've cleverly managed to sneak veggies into some of them!

Chard and Red Potato Omelet (GF)

2 Tbsp peanut oil

½ tsp cumin seeds

½ cup [70 g] finely chopped red onion

1 tsp minced ginger

¼ tsp ground turmeric

4 small red potatoes, sliced into ¼ in [6 mm] thick rounds

½ tsp kosher salt

3 large chard leaves, thinly sliced

6 eggs, whisked

¼ tsp cayenne

I love eggs. They're so versatile, I see no reason why they should be restricted to breakfast. An omelet can make a quick, tasty lunch or an easy dinner; you just have to do something a bit special to elevate it. For instance, this recipe uses red potatoes and chard to add body, while the aromatic spices uplift the whole dish.

SERVES 4 TO 6

Preheat the broiler.

Heat the oil in a cast-iron skillet over medium heat and add the cumin seeds. When they're done popping, add the onion and sauté over high heat until the onion turns dark brown, 3 to 4 minutes. Now add the ginger and turmeric, stir for 30 seconds, then add the potatoes and salt. Toss well, turn the heat down to medium, cover, and cook until the potatoes are tender but still hold their shape, about 5 minutes.

Stir in the chard, cover, and cook until wilted, barely a minute. Pour the eggs over the potato-chard mixture and cook, uncovered, until the bottom is set, about 2 minutes. Transfer the skillet under the broiler to cook the top of the omelet and wait until some attractive golden brown spots appear, about a minute or two. Remove from the oven, sprinkle with the cayenne, and serve immediately.

> **TIP:** Finishing off an omelet under the broiler is probably the cleverest kitchen hack ever. There's no disaster-prone flipping. As a bonus, the broiler puffs up your omelet beautifully while cooking it to perfection.

> **SERVING TIP:** I like to serve this alongside a simple roasted tomato salad: Since the broiler is on anyway, roast some halved tomatoes under it, and serve them on some Boston lettuce dressed with balsamic vinegar and olive oil.

Green Onion Omelet with a Curry Sauce (GF)

From trance to jazz to oldies, Goa has a terrific live music scene. With a demanding business and young kids, we still managed a few nights out (thanks, Grandma!). But driving back home at 1 a.m. makes you ravenous. So, like all the other stragglers, we'd stop at a food truck under a flickering streetlamp for one of Goa's most endearing—and enduring—late-night snacks: ros omelet. *Ros* means curry; the dish originated as a breakfast of leftovers, with the previous night's chicken curry poured over a freshly made omelet. Add a crusty bread roll to sop up the curry, and you get one of the best late-night (early-morning?) snacks ever.

SERVES 4 TO 6

To make the curry sauce: Heat the oil in a wok until very hot and add the mustard seeds. As soon as they're done sputtering, add the yellow onion. Brown the onion, about 3 minutes, and then add the ginger, coriander, turmeric, and cayenne and stir until it smells fragrant, about 1 minute. Stir in the coconut milk, salt, and sugar and let the sauce simmer until thickened, about 5 minutes. Stir in the vinegar and simmer for another 2 minutes.

To make the omelet: In a large bowl, whisk the eggs with the green onions, chile, salt, and turmeric. Heat the oil in a cast-iron skillet and pour in the eggs. I like to make my omelets over high heat, letting the first side brown a bit. When the omelet has set on the underside and also browned, about 4 minutes, flip it over. If your omelet-flipping skills aren't up to par yet, make two smaller omelets, or simply do what I've taught my kids to do—halve the omelet right there in the pan and turn it over one half-moon at a time! You could also use the broiler trick from the Chard and Red Potato Omelet (page 132).

Pour a good dollop of the curry sauce on top of the omelet, serving the rest of the sauce alongside.

CURRY SAUCE

2 Tbsp canola oil

¼ tsp mustard seeds

½ cup [70 g] finely chopped yellow onion

1 tsp finely grated ginger

1 tsp ground coriander

½ tsp ground turmeric

¼ tsp cayenne

One 13½ oz [385 g] can coconut milk, shaken well

1 tsp kosher salt

1 tsp brown sugar

1 Tbsp apple cider vinegar

OMELET

8 eggs

¼ cup [35 g] thinly sliced green onions, white and green parts

1 green chile, seeded and minced

½ tsp kosher salt, or more as needed

¼ tsp ground turmeric

2 Tbsp coconut oil

TIP: Make a jar of this curry sauce and go crazy: Dress up boiled potatoes or steamed veggies. Or drizzle over a piece of grilled fish.

SERVING TIP: I like to serve this with a crusty bread roll or baguette, which mimics the kadak pav, or "crusty bread," of Goa very nicely.

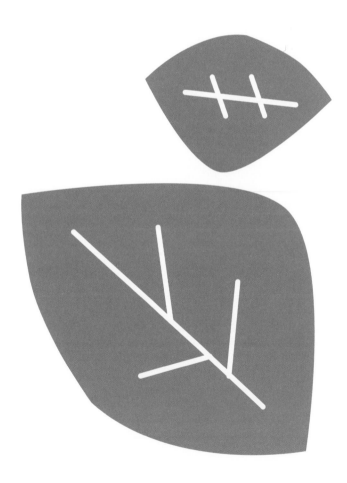

Roasted Eggs with Fennel (GF)

6 hard-boiled eggs, peeled

1 tsp kosher salt

1 Tbsp grated garlic

1 tsp cayenne

½ tsp ground turmeric

1 small fennel bulb

3 Tbsp canola oil

1 cup [200 g] thinly sliced tomatoes

I love adding interesting vegetables to a dish to get unexpected results, and here's a combination that's as unusual as it is delicious. The delicate fennel flavor goes well with the hard-boiled eggs, while the spicy tomato sauce brings the dish together.

SERVES 4 TO 6

Using a paring knife, make a vertical slit on four sides of each egg. Be careful not to make the cut too deep (see Tip). Place in a shallow bowl and sprinkle ½ tsp of the salt over them.

In a small bowl, mix the garlic, cayenne, and turmeric together to form a paste, adding a sprinkle of water if it seems too dry. Apply half of this spice paste to the eggs, carefully turning them to coat them on all sides. Reserve the remaining spice paste.

Discard any leafy fronds and halve the fennel bulb lengthwise. Place each half cut-side down and thinly slice crosswise.

Heat 2 Tbsp of the oil in a cast-iron skillet over medium heat and add the eggs, turning each egg to evenly brown all over, 3 to 5 minutes. Transfer to a plate. Add the remaining 1 Tbsp of oil to the skillet and sauté the fennel until golden brown, 3 to 4 minutes. Add the reserved spice mix and stir to cook it, about 1 minute. Now add the tomatoes and the remaining ½ tsp of salt. Cook until the tomatoes break down, about 4 minutes, and slip in the eggs. Gently turn them, scoop some of the sauce over them so they are all well coated, and turn the heat down to low. Continue cooking for 2 or 3 minutes longer so the eggs can absorb the flavors. Serve warm.

> **TIP:** Making a small incision on the eggs helps transfer the flavors inside, but be careful not to cut right through.

> **SERVING TIP:** I like to serve this with a baby spinach and red onion salad.

Salmon Two Ways (GF)

Goan fisherwomen are a photographer's delight. Loud, gaudily dressed, and laden with gold jewelry, these formidable women are ever on the lookout for a naive shopper. But they'd quickly give up when they spotted their nemesis: my mother-in-law, with her nose for the freshest fish. She would save the most premium cuts to serve whole; she'd steam the rest with potatoes and spices to make delicious fishcakes. My recipe covers both bases so you can proudly serve the dish right after it comes out of the oven. Or you can proceed a step further to make these savory salmon cakes.

OVEN-ROASTED SALMON

2 tsp canola oil

1 lb [455 g] skinless salmon fillet

8 oz [230 g] russet potatoes

¾ cup [150 g] finely chopped tomatoes

1 tsp kosher salt

½ tsp minced garlic

½ tsp cayenne

½ tsp ground turmeric

2 Tbsp finely chopped cilantro leaves

¼ tsp ground cumin

SERVES 4

Preheat the oven to 400°F [200°C]. Brush an ovenproof dish with 1 tsp of the oil and lay out the salmon fillet. Halve the potatoes lengthwise, and then slice crosswise into very thin half-moons. Lay them attractively over the salmon, fully covering the fish. Sprinkle evenly with the tomatoes, salt, garlic, cayenne, and turmeric. Drizzle the remaining 1 tsp of oil over the top.

Cover tightly with foil and place in the preheated oven. Bake until the potato is tender and the fish flakes easily, about 10 minutes. Uncover, sprinkle with the cilantro and cumin, and serve as is, or proceed to the next recipe.

SALMON CAKES

1 recipe Oven-Roasted Salmon

½ cup [70 g] finely chopped red onion

¼ cup [10 g] finely chopped cilantro leaves

2 Tbsp minced ginger

1 Tbsp minced green chile

½ tsp cumin seeds

¼ cup [60 ml] canola oil

MAKES 6 CAKES

Cool the salmon. In a large bowl, use a fork to break up the fish and potatoes. While you're looking for a fairly homogenous mix, do not make a purée; you want to end up with a chunky mash. Add the onion, cilantro, ginger, chile, and cumin seeds and combine well. Divide the salmon mixture into six equal parts and form each one into a 4 in [10 cm] patty.

Heat the oil in a cast-iron skillet over medium heat and fry three patties at a time so as not to overcrowd the pan. Cook on both sides for about 2 minutes, until well browned. Repeat with the remaining cakes.

SERVING TIP: I like to serve the warm salmon cakes over a bed of frisée dressed with a simple white wine vinegar–mustard vinaigrette.

Curry Leaf Halibut (GF)

Four 6 oz [170 g] halibut fillets

1½ tsp kosher salt

Handful of curry leaves

1 Tbsp minced garlic

1 tsp cayenne

½ tsp ground turmeric

2 Tbsp fresh lemon juice

2 Tbsp water

Native to India, the curry leaf plant is difficult to get started, speaking from experience. But once established, it will replicate wildly with a new baby sprouting under the mother plant each time you look away. In our kitchen garden, the plants were no more than a man's height. But I've been atop an elephant in Corbett National Park in North India with my face brushing the branches of the ubiquitous curry leaf trees (and my feet brushing the ubiquitous marijuana plants, but that's another story!). While curry leaves are packed with antioxidant compounds, I adore them for their unique aroma; there is simply nothing that can replace them in Indian recipes. Get some from your local Asian or Indian market and see how well they work in this baked fish preparation.

SERVES 4

Pat the fish dry with a paper towel, place in a shallow dish, and salt the fish on both sides.

In a blender, combine the curry leaves, garlic, cayenne, turmeric, lemon juice, and water and purée. Apply the marinade to the fish, turning to coat all sides. Cover and place in the refrigerator for at least 20 minutes and up to overnight.

Preheat the oven to 400°F [200°C]. Line a baking sheet with foil and transfer the halibut fillets to it. Place in the oven and bake until the fish flakes easily, about 15 minutes.

> **TIP:** Save a few curry leaves to crush into your next margarita for an amazing Indian variation, as my husband does.

> **SERVING TIP:** I like to serve this with roasted red potatoes with garlic, and a green salad with cherry tomatoes and baby cucumbers.

Flat Fish Curry (GF)

1 lb [455 g] sole fillets

1½ tsp kosher salt

½ tsp ground turmeric

1 cup [140 g] finely chopped yellow onion

2 Tbsp fresh lemon juice

1 Tbsp minced garlic

1 tsp ground cumin

½ tsp cayenne

2 Tbsp coconut oil

One 13½ oz [385 g] can coconut milk, shaken well

1 cup [240 ml] water

1 green chile, halved lengthwise

In Goa, where time moves at a glacial pace, "making lunch" can easily take up your entire morning, especially if the day's fish is lepo, a local flat fish similar to sole. First, you have to peel off the leathery skin; we're talking two dozen small, stubborn fish clinging to their sticky skins, for a family of four. After the cleaning ordeal, you have to manually grind your curry paste on the rogdo, a heavy stone grinder. Sounds exhausting, but many working home cooks have found shortcuts; they get the fish skinned at the fish market, and blenders make short work of the curry pastes. I must confess that I failed to earn my fish-cleaning stripes, choosing to support the entrepreneurial fish cleaners at the market instead.

SERVES 4

Rub the sole fillets with ½ tsp of the salt and the turmeric and set aside in the refrigerator.

Using a blender, blend ½ cup [70 g] of the onion, the lemon juice, garlic, cumin, and cayenne together to a fine paste.

Heat the oil in a wok over medium heat and sauté the remaining ½ cup [70 g] of onion until softened but still white, 2 to 3 minutes. Add the onion-spice paste and sauté for 2 minutes more. Add the coconut milk, water, chile, and the remaining 1 tsp of salt, bring to a simmer, and cook for 2 minutes. Gently slip the fish in and shake the pan to settle the fillets into the curry. Continue simmering for another 4 to 5 minutes, until the fish is fully cooked and flakes easily with a fork. Serve hot.

> **SERVING TIP:** I like to serve this with steamed broccoli and a gingery apple chutney.

Mustard Shrimp (GF)

1 lb [455 g] medium shrimp, peeled and deveined

1 tsp ground turmeric

1 tsp cayenne

1 tsp kosher salt

MUSTARD SAUCE
1 Tbsp mustard seeds

1 Tbsp minced green chile

1 Tbsp minced ginger

1 Tbsp minced garlic

¼ cup [60 ml] hot water

2 Tbsp mustard oil

1 cup [140 g] sliced red onion

1 tsp kosher salt

½ tsp sugar

½ cup [120 ml] water

¼ cup [10 g] chopped cilantro leaves

Shrimp has a natural sweetness that pairs surprisingly well with the pungent flavor of mustard. Here I use both mustard seeds and mustard oil to create a dish that's spicy in a delicious wasabi-like way. You do have to wait for the mustard seeds to soak, but once that happens, everything comes together in a snap. A cool salad of delicate lettuce and citrus fruit works well as an accompaniment.

SERVES 4

Rinse and pat dry the shrimp and place in a medium bowl. Mix in the turmeric, cayenne, and 1 tsp of salt and toss. Set aside, covered, in the refrigerator while you make the mustard sauce.

To make the mustard sauce: In a medium bowl, mix together the mustard seeds, chile, ginger, garlic, and hot water and soak for a minimum of 30 minutes. Then, using a blender, purée the mustard mixture to a smooth paste.

When you're ready to cook the shrimp, heat the oil in a wok over medium-high heat and sauté the onion until golden brown, about 5 minutes. Add the mustard paste and sauté for about 2 minutes. Mix in the shrimp, 1 tsp of salt, and the sugar. Add the water and cook, uncovered, until the shrimp are done and the sauce has thickened a bit, about 5 minutes. Stir in the cilantro and serve hot.

> **SERVING TIP:** I like to serve this with glazed carrots, and a pear and endive salad.

Thali Shrimp (GF)

1 lb [455 g] medium shrimp, peeled but tails intact

1½ tsp kosher salt

1 tsp ground turmeric

1 tsp cayenne

½ cup [70 g] rice flour

¼ cup [60 ml] canola oil

Around 1:00 p.m. on weekdays, all of Goa is suffused with the aroma of frying fish. Office workers pour out onto the streets, their noses leading them to their preferred thali, or "rice curry," joint. For many Goans, lunch is never complete without fried seafood; the day's catch could be whole sardines, buttery ladyfish, bony boyfish, mackerel, kingfish sliced into ever-thinner steaks as the market price increases, or even pricier shrimp, which will set you back a few extra rupees. Choose the shrimp thali, and you'll get a spicier curry and juicy pan-fried shrimp, simply adorned with turmeric and cayenne. When I make this dish at home in the States, the aroma of the frying shrimp creates instant nostalgia for Goan lunches.

SERVES 4

Rinse and pat dry the shrimp. Sprinkle with the salt, turmeric, and cayenne and set aside while you prep the frying oil. Place the rice flour on a plate.

Heat the oil in a cast-iron skillet over medium heat until it begins to ripple. Coat the shrimp in the flour, turning to cover all sides. Add the shrimp to the hot oil and fry in batches, taking care not to overcrowd the skillet. Cook the shrimp for about 1 minute on each side, until opaque and curled. Serve immediately.

> **SERVING TIP:** I like to serve this as finger food at my backyard parties on warm summer days with some chilled beer, but of course you could also serve it with the Flat Fish Curry (page 142) and steamed rice, as they would in Goa.

Masala Mackerel

(GF)

Two 1 lb [455 g] whole mackerel

2 Tbsp apple cider vinegar

1 Tbsp grated ginger

1 Tbsp grated garlic

1 Tbsp cayenne

1½ tsp kosher salt

1 tsp ground turmeric

20 curry leaves

2 Tbsp coconut oil

Lemon wedges, for serving

During my ten years in coastal Goa, I discovered and cooked all kinds of fish: from the Arabian Sea, the local rivers, and paddy fields—yes, paddy fields! Many of these fields are connected to the rivers via a series of bunds or embankments, and fish find their way in during the rice-growing season when the fields are flooded. When the fields are drained, the entire village shows up to buy the trapped fish. All very exciting, but my favorite fish remains the humble mackerel. It's the perfect fish: no scales and just one central bone, so it's easy to clean. And mackerel is not just delicious; it's full of healthy omega-3 fatty acids. Plus, it's plentiful and inexpensive, so what's not to like?

SERVES 4

Preheat the oven to 400°F [200°C]. Line a rimmed baking sheet with aluminum foil.

Pat the fish dry and place on the prepared baking sheet.

In a small bowl, mix together the vinegar, ginger, garlic, cayenne, salt, and turmeric and smear the spice paste on both sides of the fish, taking care to apply inside the belly cavity too.

Stack the curry leaves, roll up as tightly as you can, and slice the leaves into thin strips. Sprinkle the curry leaf ribbons all over the fish and then drizzle 1 Tbsp of oil over each fish.

Bake for 25 minutes, until the fish flakes easily. Turn on the broiler and briefly broil until the mackerel gets a little browned, about 3 minutes.

Serve with the lemon wedges.

> **SERVING TIP:** I like to serve this with sweet potato oven fries and a garlicky mayo dip.

Spicy Red Pickled Chicken (GF)

1½ lb [680 g] boneless, skinless chicken thighs

¾ cup plus 2 Tbsp [210 ml] white vinegar

3 Tbsp cayenne

2 Tbsp minced ginger

1½ Tbsp ground turmeric

1 Tbsp plus 1 tsp kosher salt

1 Tbsp minced garlic

6 Tbsp [90 ml] mustard oil

2 tsp mustard seeds

As I've said before, Indians love bold flavors. And Indian pickles are their secret weapon to perk up a simple dal and rice or a bowl of bland veggies. A spoonful of pickles makes the whole meal a lively affair. Everything is pickled, and every region has its own recipes. Indian grocery stores have aisles full of bottled pickles, from fruit to veggies, chiles to greens like sorrel, to roots like ginger and turmeric. Meat and seafood pickles, less common, are from the meat-eating regions of India. Here's my own flavor-blasting pickled chicken. Remember that it's meant to be eaten in small quantities alongside a bigger meal, so the recipe contains more heat, vinegar, and oil than you might expect.

SERVES 4 TO 6

Rinse and pat dry the chicken thighs. Trim any fat and cut the chicken into ¼ in [6 mm] pieces. Place in a medium bowl and set aside.

In a blender, blend together the vinegar, cayenne, ginger, turmeric, salt, and garlic to create a smooth paste. Add this to the chicken in the bowl and stir to coat the chicken well. Cover and set aside in the refrigerator for at least 1 hour and up to 24 hours.

Heat the oil in a wok over medium heat until rippling. Add the mustard seeds, and after they're done sputtering, add the chicken along with all the marinade. Stir well and cook until the red masala darkens, the moisture has evaporated, and you can see the oil separate—this is an indication that the masala is properly cooked—10 to 12 minutes. Remove from the heat, and once cooled, bottle in a clean glass jar. This pickle will keep in the refrigerator for 1 week.

SERVING TIP: I like to serve this with rice congee (which is a thing in India too!) and wilted spinach.

Southern Chicken Stew (GF)

1 lb [455 g] boneless, skinless chicken breasts (see Tip)

2 Tbsp coconut oil

1 green chile, quartered lengthwise

30 curry leaves

1½ cups [210 g] chopped yellow onions (½ in [13 mm] dice)

2 Tbsp thinly sliced garlic

12 oz [340 g] russet potatoes, peeled and cut into 1 in [2.5 cm] cubes

¼ cup [50 g] julienned ginger

1½ tsp kosher salt

1 tsp ground coriander

One 13½ oz [385 g] can coconut milk, shaken well

This dish, popular in the southern state of Kerala, may challenge your idea of a chicken curry. First, it has a creamy white appearance, partly due to the absence of turmeric. Second, in a country that loves heat, it is intentionally prepared light and mild. But it's delicious all the same, which is why it was perennially on the menu at my cafés in Goa. My version adds potatoes, so you can serve it as you would normally serve a stew.

SERVES 4 TO 6

Cut the chicken breasts into 1 in [2.5 cm] cubes.

Heat the oil in a wok over medium heat and add the chile; be careful—this may make you cough. Then add the curry leaves, onions, and garlic and sauté until lightly browned, about 4 minutes. Add the potatoes and continue sautéing until they turn translucent, another 4 minutes.

Add the cubed chicken, ginger, and salt and mix well. Turn the heat down to low, cover, and cook for 5 minutes, until the chicken is almost done. Sprinkle in the coriander and add the coconut milk. Simmer, uncovered, for another 5 minutes so the chicken is fully cooked and the flavors have blended together. Take care not to let the stew come to a rapid boil. Serve hot.

TIP: I've used boneless breast meat here, but bone-in thighs will definitely oomph up the sauce; just increase the cooking time to 8 to 10 minutes.

SERVING TIP: I like to serve this with crusty bread and the Green Bean Peanut Salad (page 44).

Coconut Beef Stew

(GF/IP)

½ cup [40 g] dried, shredded, unsweetened coconut

2 Tbsp coriander seeds

1 Tbsp cumin seeds

2 Tbsp minced garlic

1 tsp cayenne

1 tsp ground turmeric

2½ cups [600 ml] hot water

3 Tbsp canola oil

1 cup [140 g] finely chopped yellow onion

1 lb [455 g] beef stew meat or chuck roast, cut into 1½ in [4 cm] cubes

1 cup [200 g] finely chopped tomatoes

2½ tsp kosher salt

½ tsp sugar

1 large parsnip, cut into 1½ in [4 cm] chunks

½ cup [120 ml] coconut milk

1 Tbsp white vinegar

Beef is officially banned in most states of India; however, it is culturally significant in the regional cuisine of states like Kerala and Goa. They make the most amazing beef dishes, and many Indian tourists are eager to try the "forbidden" food. In my own cafés in Goa, I'd have to prep extra orders of my beef dishes during the tourist season to satisfy our customers from the big metros. Here's a delicious, comforting beef stew that uses coconut in two ways. Toasting the dried coconut adds a nutty richness, while adding coconut milk at the end rounds off the stew with a silky smoothness.

SERVES 4

Place a cast-iron skillet over medium heat and add the coconut. Using a rubber spatula, stir the coconut constantly until lightly toasted, about 1 minute. Be attentive because the coconut can burn quickly. Scrape it out into a bowl.

Wipe out the skillet and toast the coriander and cumin seeds until lightly browned and aromatic, 1 to 2 minutes. Again, watch carefully as burnt seeds are bitter! Transfer the seeds to a spice grinder and cool slightly before grinding into a fine powder. Transfer the powdered spices and coconut to a blender jar, add the garlic, cayenne, turmeric, and ½ cup [120 ml] of the water and purée to a smooth paste.

Heat the oil in a wok over medium-high heat, add the onion, and sauté until dark brown, 3 to 4 minutes. Add the beef and brown on all sides, about 5 minutes. Add the tomatoes, salt, sugar, and the spice paste, mix well, and add the remaining 2 cups [475 ml] of water. Bring to a boil, turn the heat down to a simmer, and cook, covered, for 30 to 45 minutes or longer if necessary, until the beef is tender. At any point if the sauce looks too dry, add up to an extra 1 cup [240 ml] of water. Add the parsnip, stir, and continue to simmer for another 15 minutes. Stir in the coconut milk and vinegar and simmer for another 5 minutes. Serve hot.

continued

INSTANT POT: Use the Sauté function to brown the onion, then brown the beef. Then turn off the Instant Pot and mix in the tomatoes, salt, sugar, the spice paste, and only 1½ cups [360 ml] of water. Cook on the Stew setting for 30 minutes. Quick-release the pressure, add the parsnip, and turn on the Sauté function again. Cover with just a regular lid and let cook until the parsnips are tender, about 5 minutes. Stir in the coconut milk and vinegar and simmer for another 5 minutes.

TIP: Root vegetables go well with this curry. I've mentioned parsnips, but feel free to use any of your faves: turnips, carrots, rutabagas, or even potatoes.

SERVING TIP: I like to serve this with a green salad with tangerines and apples.

Lamb with Lentils

(GF/IP)

LAMB DAL

1 Tbsp grated ginger

1 Tbsp grated garlic

3 tsp kosher salt

1 tsp cayenne

1 tsp ground turmeric

1 lb [455 g] leg of lamb, cut into 1 in [2.5 cm] cubes

One 15½ oz [440 g] can cannellini beans, drained

1 bunch (10½ oz [300 g]) spinach, coarsely chopped

1½ cups [300 g] finely chopped tomatoes

½ cup [100 g] red lentils, rinsed

1 Tbsp julienned ginger

1 green chile, quartered lengthwise

1 Tbsp ground coriander

1 tsp ground cumin

2 cups [475 ml] water

BURNT ONIONS

¼ cup [60 ml] canola oil

1 large yellow onion, very thinly sliced

2 Tbsp fresh lemon juice

This dish hails from the Parsi community, who fled their native Persia after it was conquered by the Muslims in the seventh century. The recipe itself had me stumped for a while. Should it go in the dal or meat chapter? It's definitely a very satisfying dal, but it's also a lovely lamb dish! In the end, I decided to place it with the meat dishes because in India, meat is often cooked with beans and lentils, whereas the reverse isn't always true. By the way, most Indians use a pressure cooker to shorten cooking time and still get that slow-cooked flavor. So this recipe is the perfect candidate for your Instant Pot.

SERVES 4 TO 6

To make the lamb dal: In a medium bowl, mix together the grated ginger, garlic, 2 tsp of the salt, cayenne, and turmeric. Add the cubed lamb and coat with the marinade. Refrigerate for at least 20 minutes, and up to overnight.

In a large stockpot, add the beans, spinach, tomatoes, lentils, julienned ginger, chile, remaining 1 tsp of salt, the coriander, cumin, and water. Add the lamb, stir well, and set over high heat. Bring to a boil, turn the heat down to medium-low, cover, and cook until the lamb is tender and the dal is thick, 30 to 45 minutes.

While the lamb is cooking, make the burnt onions: Heat the oil over medium heat in a cast-iron skillet and fry the onions until they turn a very dark brown, just short of burnt, about 10 minutes. Drain and transfer to a paper towel; they will crisp up as they cool.

Stir the lemon juice into the lamb dal and garnish with the onions. Serve hot.

INSTANT POT: Place the marinated lamb, beans, spinach, tomatoes, lentils, julienned ginger, chile, coriander, cumin, 1 tsp of salt, and turmeric in the Instant Pot. Add only 1½ cups [360 ml] of water. Cook on the manual Pressure Cook setting on High for 15 minutes. Allow the pressure to release naturally. Proceed with the rest of the recipe.

> **SERVING TIP:** I like to serve this with mashed potatoes, saving some of the burnt onions to garnish the mash, and a simple green salad.

Roasted Lamb with Beets

(GF/IP)

3 Tbsp plain whole-milk yogurt

1 green chile, quartered lengthwise

2 Tbsp ground coriander

1 Tbsp grated ginger

1 Tbsp grated garlic

2 tsp kosher salt

1 tsp cayenne

1 tsp ground cumin

½ tsp ground turmeric

1 lb [455 g] leg of lamb, cut into 1½ in [4 cm] pieces

1 bunch (10½ oz [300 g]) beets with greens attached

2 Tbsp mustard oil

2 cups [280 g] sliced yellow onions

1½ cups [300 g] finely chopped tomatoes

1 cup [240 ml] water

Lamb is probably the most commonly eaten meat in India, where it's known as mutton, the word itself a leftover from the British. And when you order mutton, you're more likely to get goat than sheep. Although Indians love to use lamb in spicy curries and roasts, I've found that it pairs very well with sweeter flavors. In *5 Spices, 50 Dishes*, I have a recipe that combines lamb with milk and raisins. Here, beets add a lovely sweetness and, of course, rich color.

SERVES 4 TO 6

In a large bowl, mix together the yogurt, chile, coriander, ginger, garlic, salt, cayenne, cumin, and turmeric. Add the lamb and rub the marinade all over well. Cover and place in the refrigerator for 1 hour and up to overnight. The longer the lamb marinates, the better.

Preheat the oven to 400°F [200°C]. Separate the greens from the beets and rinse both well. Chop the greens finely. Peel and chop the beets into 1 in [2.5 cm] cubes. Bring a pan of water to a boil and blanch the cubed beets for 1 minute. You do not want them to cook all the way. Drain.

Heat the oil in a wok over medium-high heat and sauté the onions until they turn dark brown, about 10 minutes. Add the marinated lamb and the tomatoes and stir. Add the beets, greens, and water and transfer to an ovenproof dish. Cover, place in the oven, and bake for 1 hour. Uncover and continue baking until the lamb is meltingly tender and the sauce thickens, about 30 minutes. Serve warm.

INSTANT POT: Use the Sauté function to brown the onions. Then turn it off and mix in the marinated lamb, tomatoes, beets, and greens. Use only ¼ cup [60 ml] of water. Cook on the manual Pressure Cook setting on High for 15 minutes.

Preheat the oven to 400°F [200°C]. Once the Instant Pot has released pressure naturally, transfer the lamb to an ovenproof dish. Bake for 10 minutes or so, until the lamb is nicely browned.

SERVING TIP: I like to serve this with Black Grape Raita (page 52) and Brussels Sprouts with Fried Red Lentils (page 64). Try this combo at your holiday table.

Dry Fry Pork (GF)

1 lb [455 g] pork loin, cut into 1 in [2.5 cm] pieces

2½ tsp kosher salt

1 tsp ground turmeric

1 Tbsp cumin seeds

1 Tbsp coriander seeds

2 tsp mustard seeds

5 Tbsp [75 ml] canola oil

1 cup [140 g] finely chopped yellow onion

1 Tbsp grated ginger

1 Tbsp grated garlic

1 Tbsp minced green chile

1 Tbsp apple cider vinegar

Not commonly associated with Indian food, pork is eaten in certain parts of the country: Kerala, Coorg, Goa, and the Seven Sisters states of Northeast India, which have an amazing cuisine all their own. Here's a quick pork stir-fry for busy weeknights. If you have the time to prep a little in the morning, you can marinate the pork and quickly roast and powder the spices: I promise it won't take you more than 5 minutes to do this. Besides, the aroma of the spices will act like your second cup of coffee and jolt you awake!

SERVES 4

Put the pork in a large bowl and toss with the salt and turmeric. Set aside, covered, in the refrigerator, for at least 20 minutes and up to overnight.

In a small cast-iron skillet over medium heat, toast the cumin seeds, coriander seeds, and 1 tsp of the mustard seeds. Cool slightly and grind to a fine powder in a spice grinder.

Heat the oil in a wok over medium heat and pop the remaining 1 tsp of the mustard seeds in it. Throw in the onion and sauté until a deep brown, about 5 minutes. Add the ginger and garlic and sauté for 1 minute more. Add the pork, chile, and ground spices and sauté until well mixed. Cover and cook for 10 minutes over medium heat, uncovering to stir it up a couple of times, so nothing sticks and burns. Turn off the heat, stir in the vinegar, cover, and let sit for 5 minutes. Serve warm.

SERVING TIP: This dish is great served with steamed rice and Pink Lentils with Kale (page 110). Or serve as Indian-style tacos, with pico de gallo, baby arugula, and some corn tortillas.

Acknowledgments

We moved from Goa to Milwaukee in August 2020, right in the middle of the pandemic. The world seemed to have stopped, but it gave me time to reflect on what I would do next.

As I made cautious plans to open a café, Claire Gilhuly at Chronicle Books called me out of the blue. My first cookbook, *5 Spices, 50 Dishes*, had just gone out of print after a fourteen-year run. Would I like to write another? For someone who's happiest juggling multiple projects, it felt like sunny old times! And the familiar whirlwind began again.

The year 2021 was a blur: establishing a café in a new city, settling the kids into a new school and environment, finding a house in an insane market, and of course, writing a new cookbook. All through the chaos, my editor and spark igniter Claire Gilhuly was supportive, gentle, and patient. Vanessa Dina's fabulous design made the project exciting right from the start. Ghazalle Badiozamani's incredible photography and Jesse Szewczyk's food styling brought my recipes to life. Thank you all.

I'd also like to give a big shout-out to the hugely underrated city of Milwaukee and the folks who made us feel so welcome here; many of them have become close friends.

And last but not least, thanks to my sweet little family, without whom there is no adventure.

Index